# Voice Made Visible

*Voice Made Visible* is an exploration of voice training and performance practice based on the use and application of Multi-Octave Vocal Range techniques.

"Multi-Octave" is understood as the arsenal of sounds that exists uniquely within each human voice, beyond the comfortable average octave that we use in everyday life. In *Voice Made Visible*, Rafael Lopez-Barrantes builds on the voice work created by Alfred Wolfsohn and developed by Roy Hart and his company in France to assist students, artists, and those interested in the performing arts with their vocal practice. He draws from over three decades of multi-cultural performance and teaching, sharing the three fundamental pillars of his system: Fiction, News, and Body Source. This book will help readers unfold their understanding of the voice by strengthening it and inspire them to create new vocal paths for the stage, camera, and voice acting, as well as for their own personal expressive growth.

*Voice Made Visible* is an invaluable resource for students of Acting and Voice courses, as well as working performing artists.

For supplemental material, including pedagogical audio-visual clips, please visit www.barrantesvoicesystem.com.

**Rafael Lopez-Barrantes** is the creator of the Barrantes Voice System (BVS) and co-founder of the Archipelago Theater in France and the US. Rafael's work as a Spanish performer and voice teacher developed from his time acting, directing, and teaching with the Roy Hart Theatre, as well as research in traditional Japanese Noh Theater, Buddhist Shomio, and Spanish Flamenco. He was a faculty member at the National School of Puppetry Arts in France from 1984 to 1992, Duke University from 1992 to 2007, and the American Dance Festival from 1992 to 2015. Since 2007, he has been a full-time faculty member in the School of Theater at the California Institute of the Arts teaching the Barrantes Voice System to MFA and BFA students. Between 2010 and 2016, Rafael served as the Associate Director of Performance for the CalArts School of Theater and in 2018 conceived the House of Voices initiative. Rafael is committed to the development of the BVS teacher certification program for CalArts alumni.

# Voice Made Visible

## Multi-Octave Voice Training and Techniques for Performers

### Rafael Lopez-Barrantes

Edited by Grace Leneghan

Illustrated by
Aaron Lopez-Barrantes

NEW YORK AND LONDON

Designed cover image: Aaron Lopez-Barrantes

First published 2024
by Routledge
605 Third Avenue, New York, NY 10158

and by Routledge
4 Park Square, Milton Park, Abingdon, Oxon, OX14 4RN

*Routledge is an imprint of the Taylor & Francis Group, an informa business*

© 2024 Rafael Lopez-Barrantes
Illustrations © 2024 Aaron Lopez-Barrantes

The right of Rafael Lopez-Barrantes to be identified as author of this work has been asserted in accordance with sections 77 and 78 of the Copyright, Designs and Patents Act 1988.

All rights reserved. No part of this book may be reprinted or reproduced or utilised in any form or by any electronic, mechanical, or other means, now known or hereafter invented, including photocopying and recording, or in any information storage or retrieval system, without permission in writing from the publishers.

*Trademark notice*: Product or corporate names may be trademarks or registered trademarks, and are used only for identification and explanation without intent to infringe.

*Library of Congress Cataloging-in-Publication Data*
Names: Lopez-Barrantes, Rafael, author. | Leneghan, Grace, editor. | Lopez-Barrantes, Aaron, illustrator.
Title: Voice made visible : voice training and performance practices with multi-octave vocal range techniques / Rafael Lopez-Barrantes ; edited by Grace Leneghan ; illustrated by Aaron Lopez-Barrantes.
Description: New York, NY : Routledge, 2024. |
Includes index. Identifiers: LCCN 2023014608 (print) |
LCCN 2023014609 (ebook) | ISBN 9781032451794 (hardback) |
ISBN 9781032451787 (paperback) | ISBN 9781003376842 (ebook)
Subjects: LCSH: Voice culture.
Classification: LCC PN4162 .L66 2024 (print) |
LCC PN4162 (ebook) | DDC 808.5–dc23/eng/20230707
LC record available at https://lccn.loc.gov/2023014608
LC ebook record available at https://lccn.loc.gov/2023014609

ISBN: 978-1-032-45179-4 (hbk)
ISBN: 978-1-032-45178-7 (pbk)
ISBN: 978-1-003-37684-2 (ebk)

DOI: 10.4324/9781003376842

Typeset in Optima
by Newgen Publishing UK

Access the Support Material: www.barrantesvoicesystem.com

*To Alfred Wolfsohn, Roy Hart, the Roy Hart
Theatre, all my pupils, and especially to my sons
Aaron and Samuel*

*Knowledge is a rumor until the body knows it.*
– An ancient proverb from the Asaro Tribe in Papua New Guinea

# Contents

Acknowledgements     ix

Introduction     1

1   Beginnings     4
    *In the Beginning Was Sound*   4
    *The Foundations of My Work*   5
    *My Own Epiphany*   6

2   Voice Made Visible     9
    *The De-Colonization of the Voice*   9
    *"I Want to Be Someone Like Somebody Else Was Once" and the Multi-Octave Voice*   11
    *Voice Made Visible*   14

3   The Prerequisites: Fiction and News     16
    *Fiction*   16
    *News*   23

4   Sound Grounding     28
    *The Eyes*   28
    *Head Resonators*   32
    *The Mouth*   35
    *The Pharynx*   37
    *The Thorax*   51
    *The Diaphragm ("The Power Tool")*   57
    *The Abdomen*   62
    *The Pelvis*   65

## 5   The Industry of Breath and Alignment  78
   On Breath  78
   Alignment  94
   Shower Mouth  97
   Gills and Intercostal Awakening  101
   Three Basic Tongue Positions  110
   Support of Sound with Diaphragm  117
   Four Times Eight  120
   Voice Like Concrete: Shomio  123
   Acoustic Levels  129
   Foo Dog Experiment  137

## 6   The Foundational Pillars: The Body Sources  142
   From Chaos to Order: The Body Source  142
   Earth  144
   Broken Earth  148
   Strong Wood  154
   Soft Wood  158
   Broken Wood  160
   Epic Hollow Wood  162
   Lyric Hollow Wood  164
   Metal  165
   Broken Metal  169
   Air  172
   Water  177
   The Scream  182

## 7   Training  186
   Grotesque  186
   Building Your Training Session  189
   Eclipse Yourself: The Task  196
   On Connection  200

   Conclusion: The Universe in a Lid . . .  207

   Glossary  209
   Index  218

# Acknowledgements

Writing this book has been a deep pleasure for me, in large part because of the encouragement and assistance many people – especially my students – have given me throughout the years.

I would initially like to thank my first teachers Roy Hart, Richard Armstrong, Barry Coghlan, and Saule Ryan – and most deeply Marita Gunter for her patience and generous energy over 15 years of her profound teachings. I am also most indebted to the late Alfred Wolfsohn (1896–1962). Without his vision and perseverance, the work I have done and developed would have never seen the light.

I want to thank the many people whom I have worked alongside and crossed paths with over the years. They come from the worlds of arts, sciences, and human sciences, but most importantly from the vast universe of life.

My heartfelt recognition goes to those colleagues and professionals whose individual techniques and approaches helped guide my inner compass. Thanks to them, I learned that if one is sufficiently open to experience, all roads *can* indeed lead to Rome. *Gracias* to the following: Abbot Dr Fujita of the Daienin temple (Koyasan, Wakayama Prefecture, Japan); Robert Courbon, for his acupuncture instruction; Claire Heggen for her heart and body knowledge; Laurie McKlin for her art and body practice; Charles Reinhart, Martha Myers, Donna Faye Burchfield, and Jodee Nimerichter of American Dance Festival; Masao Yamaguchi for his mentorship, generosity, and knowledge of world theater; E. Barba, Yoshi Oida, El Toro, Marie Agnes Faure, Heide Teggeder, Akeo Kanze, Kosuke Nomura, and Travis Preston.

Adam J. Smith and Kalean Ung for their editing help and Grace Leneghan for her dedication and thorough work seen throughout my whole book. My partners Johannes Theron, Ellen Hemphill, and Maurice Boswell. My son Aaron for his illustrations and my son Samuel for his most valuable first edits. And last but not least, all my students for making me the teacher that I am.

Finally, I would like to thank Hirokazu Kosaka sensei, Master Artist in residence at the Japanese American Community Cultural Center in Los Angeles, and Tatsushige Udaka sensei of the Kongo School of Noh Theater in Kyoto, for their depth of knowledge of the disciplines of Kyudo and Noh and for how they inspired me.

# Introduction

As a 21-year-old, I dreamed of one day writing a book that would speak about my experience of the voice. Forty-two years later, as I write from a Japanese monastery while on my sabbatical semester at California Institute of the Arts (CalArts), I am finally ready to dive into my life's work by investigating, structuring, and developing decades of thoughts and lessons that I have assembled over these many years.

On March 9, 2015, I traveled to Mount Koya, Wakayama prefecture, Japan. Once I finally reached Gokurakubashi, the base of the mountain, a number of signs guided me to an unusual red and cream yellow cable car. This took me to the top of the Koya San Mountain.

I had never been in a railcar like this before. It felt like an oversized, broad, steep staircase, built at a 60° angle with large panoramic windows all around, allowing me to fully take in the spectacular view. Though it looked rather antiquated, it was clearly a very sturdy and safe "mountain ship." A gentle shake with a barely audible engine noise started to elevate me and all the other passengers up the steep mountain's slope, our backs to the mountain and our eyes down at the platform as it faded away.

I found myself thinking that this would not simply be another mountain climb. The cable car was offering me an ascension from the depths of the valley to the very peak of the mountain!

And suddenly it hit me: what a great way to begin writing my book! Every time I readjusted my body on my seat, I felt the strong pull of gravity, shifting me forward. I had never experienced anything like this. Nor had I experienced what I would describe as a strange hourglass-like optical effect. As we went up, what was

DOI: 10.4324/9781003376842-1

below us closed in like a narrowing, centripetal circle, zooming away. Simultaneously, what had been behind our backs and above us fanned out like an immense aperture, opening wide as it zoomed closer to the clouds. Straight ahead, the horizon got broader and wider, unveiling new mountain ranges. Hundreds of trees stood guard on both sides of our "mountain ship," escorting our ascent.

A few minutes later, we arrived at the top of *Koya San Mountain*. The valleys deep below us were now hidden by a sea of soft, rippling clouds that transformed the mountains into distant islands. The wide-open sky at the top of the mountain was an arresting winter-crystal blue.

I was transported elsewhere. I knew: *I will be able to write here*. I have come to this particular place in Japan because of the fierce inspiration I felt the first time I heard Shomio. It was the summer of 1984 in Tokyo. Jodo Buddhist reverend, Horyu Haneda, introduced me to this soul-stirring style of devotional chanting. Now, 31 years later, I have returned to Japan. This time, however, I am coming to the very cradle and repository of the Shingon Buddhist Shomio tradition. Its founder Kukai, later known as Kobho Daishi, established it here during the ninth century. It is in his headquarters that I will get up well before sunrise to start the day. As I sat and listened to the Shomio chanting, and as I closed my eyes to meditate, I began to put order to the thoughts, notes, and writings of my last 42 years.

This book is the result of innumerable hours spent taking voice lessons, giving them, preparing them, dreaming about them, and pondering about them. It is also the outcome of many failures, bumps on the road, and successes in the unfinished process of becoming a voice teacher.

*Voice Made Visible* is an exploration for voice training and performing practice based on the use and application of Multi-Octave Vocal Range techniques. "Multi-Octave" is understood as that "arsenal of sounds" that exists uniquely within each human voice, beyond the comfortable average octave that we use in everyday life.

You will find the essential terms in the book **bolded** when first introduced and developed further in the Glossary. In addition to this book, please visit: www.barrantesvoicesystem.com for supplemental material including pedagogical audio-visual clips to complement what you will read here.

My hope is that this manual will assist you in your practice and open your understanding of the voice, strengthen it, and inspire you to create new paths.

Thank you very much for reading it.

Rafael Lopez-Barrantes
*Koya San, Wakayama, Japan*

# Chapter 1
# Beginnings

### In the Beginning Was Sound

> Be not afeared. The isle is full of noises. Sounds, and sweet airs, that give delight and hurt not. Sometimes a thousand twangling instruments will hum about mine ears; and sometimes voices, that, if I then had wak'd after long sleep, will make me sleep again; and then, in dreaming the clouds methought would open and show riches ready to drop upon me, that, when I waked I cried to dream again.
>
> Shakespeare, *The Tempest* 3.2, Caliban

The notion of "**Multi-Octave Vocal Range**" stems from the observation that there is far more to the voice than the sounds we hear and make daily. There is a vital gap between the sounds available to us as human animals, and our ability – let alone willingness – to express these sounds.

The use of the voice in our culture appears to rest on the tenet of achieving maximum effect with minimum effort. On the other hand, when we think of producing voice for the stage, the opposite should be true: "invest maximum effort to achieve what seemingly looks effortless."

With the advent of Modernism, our ability to get drunk in thought and chatter has increased considerably; but while we can engage in small talk until we are blue in the face, the truth is we do this to muffle pain, cover hurt, and deaden the anxieties inherent to the human condition. While we have learned how to develop sophisticated forms of abstract thought (how to fly to the moon, how to build a nuclear submarine), our ability to draw upon sensorial, experiential, and emotional intelligence is lacking.

DOI: 10.4324/9781003376842-2

Imagine if we could better understand the disconnect between our technological prowess and our animal nature! While many of us know how to build a website, for example, our ability to decrypt, liberate, and communicate the more primordial aspects of our being seems to remain elusive.

One way to remedy this situation is by putting our effort and abilities toward connecting to a basic universal humanity. Brigitte Gauthier wrote about Pina Bausch's work of the importance of erasing one's cultural and social differences in artmaking.

Performance, being such an efficient vehicle for understanding our human experience, condition, and emotions, appears to be the ideal tool for potentially closing that disconnect. As a performer, I am convinced that the voice can bridge the gap between the noise of modernity and the connection to our more primal selves. In the beginning was sound. We must not only hear it, but also listen to it.

## The Foundations of My Work

The work developed in this book has its roots in the work originated by the visionary Alfred Wolfsohn (1896–1962).

Born in Germany, Wolfsohn became a singing and voice teacher. He served in the First World War where he survived the seminal experience of being buried alive in the trenches amongst the bodies of dying soldiers. The emotional force and power of the sounds he heard then led him to explore with his own voice and to develop a new understanding of the power of the human voice and what lies behind it. The rise of Nazism in Germany made A.W., as he was endearingly called then, seek asylum in London. Over the years several pupils gathered around him researching and exploring their own voices beyond the four basic existing traditional vocal registers: soprano, alto, tenor, and bass. His work on the voice became intimately connected and inspired by human psychology, Jung, and disciplined self-study. A unique and very progressive modern understanding of the voice was born.

After his death, one of his pupils, Roy Hart (1926–1975) took the lead on the work, adding a strong theater component to what Wolfsohn had previously created and developed. Over the years, the work became better known and attracted many people. In the mid-sixties, with the presence of 40 people, the **Roy Hart Theatre** was created. In July 1974, the company moved to the South of France, to the Chateau de Malerargues: an abandoned hotel in the heart of the Cevennes mountains on a former seventeenth-century silk farm in the Languedoc-Roussillon, near the towns of Nimes, Avignon, and Montpellier, and an important center of "La Resistance" in France during World War II.

I spent 16 meaningful years of my life there. The Chateau felt to be a real hands-on, international, "utopian" village. Hard work but meaningful. This life adventure still informs what I do and how I do it. This chapter of my life was loaded with joys, struggles, discoveries, contradictions, and growth, yet driven by the vision of this multicultural, theater community where its 40 members created, researched, studied, and experienced the possibilities of the voice. This school of life and of theater helped me to refine, build and develop what later in my life has become my vision, culminating in the creation of the Barrantes Voice System.

**My Own Epiphany**

In March of 1971, I was a third-year law student at the Universidad Complutense de Madrid. As I was about to start dinner that night, my friend Juanjo called me. "Rafael, come! In 30 minutes, there is a performance that you have to see at the Teatro de la Zarzuela."

I left my dinner untouched on the table and ran. The performance "And," by the Roy Hart Theatre, was part of Madrid's International Theater Festival that year. As I watched it, I became spellbound, paralyzed in my seat for almost two hours. Though I had seen plenty of theater before, I had never experienced anything like this. The entire piece was performed with "pre-verbal" sounds, songs, and phonemes . . . no words. And yet, I seemed to understand everything on a visceral, emotional, universal level. This was an epiphany for me. My life changed forever. That night I experienced the protean nature of the voice. My life took a turn in that very moment. That night I knew I would join the Roy Hart Theatre as soon as I finished law school (which would also mark the end of my law career). I became passionate about the voice. From then on and through years of research, practice, and study, I discovered the plethora of possibilities contained in what we refer to in the West as the Multi-Octave Vocal Range.

I joined the Roy Hart Theatre in London on February 24, 1974. At the time, the company was a very hermetic and tightly knit ensemble of people from many nationalities. We worked, lived, and created theater together, and by July 1 that year, seven of us, "The Magnificent Seven," had begun to move the company to France. After a period of six months, all 40 of us were living in the Chateau de Malerargues, our headquarters in the Midi of France.

During those years I worked a variety of jobs. I painted many walls, became a plaster finishing master, retiled roofs, translated papers, cleaned kennels, combed many high end "silver match" poodles (which I really did not care for), taught children, became a sous-chef and later a chef, became a tour manager and a grant administrator, took theater and dance workshops, picked apples, chestnuts and grapes, learned the technical aspects of the stage, became a voice teacher, gave workshops, traveled the world, joined the faculty of the National School of Puppetry, acted, directed, and co-founded the Archipelago Theater France with my partner, Johannes Theron. By 1988, I became the wealthiest man in the world: the father of my extraordinary twin sons Aaron and Samuel.

Two years later, in August 1990, I moved with my own family to the United States. I worked for 15 years at the Theater Studies Department of Duke University (North Carolina) and the American Dance Festival, where I taught Multi-Octave Vocal Range techniques to dancers and choreographers.

I acted, directed, co-founded Archipelago Theater USA with my partner, Ellen Hemphill, and created Celebrations Inc., which became a very successful business producing and enhancing high-end events through the arts and design for notables like President Clinton, Michael Jordan, Yoyo Ma, and Luciano Pavarotti, among others. The government of Spain appointed me as Honorary Consul of Spain in 2000 (2000–2005), and in 2007 I moved to Los Angeles, California, after being offered a teaching position at the Theater School at California Institute of the Arts. I served as Associate Director of Performance for a number of years and continue teaching graduate and undergraduate students the Multi-Octave Vocal Range Technique now known as the Barrantes Voice System.

Parallel to my life in the Roy Hart Theatre, I focused my research on the study and practice of two ancient cultural traditions where the voice and gesture play a profound role. One is represented by Spanish Cante Jondo (Deep Flamenco Singing), and the other relates to Japanese traditional Noh Theater and **Shomio** Buddhist chanting.

I sojourned twice to Tokyo; the first in 1984 when I was invited by theater anthropologist and professor Masao Yamaguchi (1931–2013) of Tokyo Gaikokugo Daigaku. Yamaguchi San introduced me to the writings of Zeami, who along with his father Kannami, are considered the originators of Noh Theater (fourteenth century). There is no question that his writings and Noh Theater have deeply influenced my approach to process and performance.

It was also on that visit that I heard for the first time Shomio, an ancient ninth-century chanting practice belonging to the **Shingon Buddhist** sect initiated by Kobodaishi Gobyo. I am fully indebted to Mr. Horyu Haneda who introduced me to his Jodo sect Shomio style. Shomio's impact on my life has been a very deep and inspiring source ever since, leading me to live in the Daienin Monastery, in Koya San, to practice Shomio at its birthplace.

My second visit to Japan was in 1987 when my partner Ellen Hemphill obtained a grant from the Asian Cultural Council in New York, which enabled us to travel to research the Japanese traditional forms of Noh and Kyogen. Both visits were crucial for developing my teaching and stage techniques. Not only did it open me up as an actor, a teacher, and a researcher, but it also guided me as a director. Through these seminal experiences, I created several works of theater with both my companies, Archipelago Theater France and Archipelago Theater USA.

My process all those years was fundamentally informed not only by studying, but also by the inclusion of empirical, artistic, and experiential research.

*Voice Made Visible* addresses the educational, aesthetic, and philosophical principles that inform my current pedagogic method and artistic practice.

# Chapter 2
# Voice Made Visible

### The De-Colonization of the Voice

For decades, I have been pondering the work of the actor and the inherent transformational power of the voice. The common saying, *"In the beginning was the word"* has always bothered me due to the implicit supremacy granted to language. I'd like to propose:

> *"In the beginning there was sound."*

*Sound* is a primordial utterance. We are born in sound. The first thing we do when we enter this world is scream as we take our first breath. There is something about the phrasing of "the word" in the original proverb that seems "divisive," while we cannot say the same thing about sound. *Sound* precedes the apparition of words. Sound has the benefit of acting as a proto language, while "the word" is a highly sophisticated specialization of sound that helps to differentiate groups of people through language and dialect. We are both fascinated and scared of each other. While words create boundaries, sound connects us all.

In sound, our inner ear not only listens and discerns carefully, a matter of fight or flight animal response, but deciphers the meaning behind that sound without interference or the intermediary of words. I would guess that the first human animal that expressed tender feelings for another did so through singing sounds, utterances, and touch, rather than words.

If we believe that *"In the beginning there was sound,"* then we can bridge the disconnect between words and meaning with others, as well as become less foreign to ourselves. The word *language* has "colonized" us by driving our voices on remote control. Even though sound existed before the appearance of the word, we live under the tyranny and imperialistic inflation of the word.[1] We must remind ourselves that the voice is emotion and experience, not just a platform or a vehicle for trafficking words. We need to return to a state in which the voice itself is primary in expression, superseding language, rather than the voice remaining a "colonized" servant to words. We must decolonize the voice from language's supremacy so that we can restore to the word its emotional, experiential, and energetic powers.

Each individual, and hence each voice, is unique. Each voice contains within itself its own imprint. What if we considered the voice as an ecosystem unto itself composed of an ensemble of textures, elements, and identities? Suffice it to think of (and this is not a metaphor) how voraciously the industry is pursuing methods to identify each and every voice in order to open doors, windows, unlock passwords, bank accounts, etc. The price of convenience at the hands of technological progress is the usurpation of our vocal individuality.

What interests me in the Multi-Octave Vocal Range is its potential to give back to the voice its protean nature as an instrument of expression and communication versus an instrument of power. I am thinking of "power" as all the overzealous political, ideological, and religious (both historic and contemporary) examples of voice power.

What the Barrantes Voice System strives for in the voice is its intrinsic diversity and versatility. As individuals, we experience the voice as something impermanent, much like spring mist, or insubstantial like an open sky; however, as a man of theater and as a voice pedagogue, I strive to see the voice as something very real and material. I consider the voice as a holistic mass, which includes muscles, cartilage, mucosae, nerves, bones, viscera, and air. Yet together, it does not occupy any one fixed place in the body, but rather many and none at the same time.

I long for the voice to have as much of a substance as possible so that I can create and render it visible to the audience. Voice is a theater,[2] or as Roland Barthes referred to it while speaking of his love for German lieder: "a kitchen of reflected emotion." This is a very inspiring quote for me. It brings forth the notion of materiality and tangibility of the voice or the dish in question with its variety of ingredients, possible ways of cooking, temperatures, condiments, etc., as well as the notion of emotional transformation that happens as we admire the final "dish" (the final vocal product). Hence, the voice can be perceived as a substance, as sustenance, and as consumption. Voice as tapas, appetizers, entrees, and desserts. Voice as a metaphoric ingestion of what we experience when we listen "ad libitum" to our favorite lullabies, chants, songs, and arias.

Do you remember the last time you listened to one of your favorite voices? For me this is Katherine Ferrier, Eartha Kitt, Tom Waits, El Agujetas, Janis Joplin, Maria Callas, Thomas Quasthoff, The Beatles, Billie Holiday, Mahalia Jackson, and the Shite in Japanese Noh theater. As soon as the voice is heard that voice is physically gone, yet still works inside of us, sustaining us and creating memory.

How many times have we wanted to say, "Sing it again, please!" to our favorite singer? This is a futile attempt to hold onto it and make it ours. We want to hear it once more so that our spirit and memories are nourished over and over again by hearing our favorite voices, and yet, what an extraordinary paradox. The voice is at the same time substance and transparency; it allows us to see through.

It connects us both to the core of experience and emotion, as well as to the mystery. The voice is always ephemeral in its presence, however forever lasting in its essence.

## "I Want to Be Someone Like Somebody Else Was Once" and the Multi-Octave Voice

Just like the performer it resides in, the voice is a nomad "par excellence." It travels and moves constantly with our emotional fleeting moods. The human voice is constantly adjusting and transforming its fluid frontiers. Now it appears and then suddenly is gone. It is evanescent, ephemeral, and hard to pin down: a fugitive of sorts. However, the moment we can pinpoint the consistent source of the voice, be it emotional, physical, or imaginative, and learn to repeat it, we become distinctly more ourselves.

The voice is not a simple instrument existing "out there" and made from a particular material, but rather a complex one produced from human substances and from the depths of human experience. In fact, it is not outrageous to say that the voice is made of the same "stuff as dreams are made on." The voice is a fluctuant, sensitive, and delicate instrument to maintain because it must be tuned not only with the body, but also with the mind and the spirit. There is a myriad of neurobiological complexities at work to make it function properly at the right time, with the right emotion, and for the right reason.

The voice I am talking about is the one that stands behind Peter Handke's aphorism in his masterful play *Kaspar*, in which the titular character repeats ad libitum:

"*I want to be someone like somebody else was once.*"

*Kaspar* is loosely based on the historical figure **Kaspar Hauser**, a German boy who claimed to be raised in total isolation, deprived of language itself, and then suddenly appeared at a Nuremberg square one day armed with only a single sentence (that he apparently did not even understand the meaning of). He became the ward of a well-known socialite lawyer, who educated and socialized him toward assimilation.

If we breakdown the sentence above from Handke's play, we uncover a few fundamentals:

"*I want to be someone . . .*"

He, Kaspar, wants to communicate and wants to come into existence. Kaspar not only wants to re-establish the connection with himself prior to his socialization, but he also wants to include those different "somebody's" that we all experience during the unfolding of our lives:

"*. . . like somebody else was once.*"

By verbalizing "*I want to be someone like somebody else was once,*" we can deduce that Kaspar (you, me, the actor) finds himself in the ideal circumstances so that he is able to act. And of course, even though it might be obvious, by virtue of stating these needs, he is expressing himself. Kaspar wants to connect to something which he intuits has always been inside of him, and without stating that desire, no action will manifest.

Saying such a phrase–statement tells us that he has created a favorable environment where things can naturally happen and develop. He is right on target regarding the relational aspect of the voice because his fervent desire to express himself and to communicate with "the other" exists already. Since he has a longing for connection, he might stand a chance to materialize the statement he first uttered.

Kaspar's need to connect with his previous self is how I see the voice. In this context, all Kaspar's "somebody" translates to the many textures that are revealed by the Multi-Octave Voice, that vocal territory that remains outside the well-known one octave voice framework we hear and use in our everyday lives. In expanding the vocal range, we open to multiple dormant identities and expressions contained within ourselves. In view of this, I would like to suggest that we are repositories of personal as well as ancestral emotions and experiences. Today we experience ourselves as singular and unique individuals, but if we look back to our parents and parents' parents, etc., there is an interminable lineage of individuals, as well as worlds of sounds, that came before us.

The Multi-Octave Voice could be regarded as the connective tissue of the imaginative, emotional, cognitive, and spiritual chambers of our being; a **"proto voice"** that is accessible and identifiable by all individuals regardless of culture, age, gender, or any other social construct available. We could even refer to it as the "objective voice" in the sense of a voice that is *universal*. It exists within every individual, beyond linguistic and cultural differences.

The Multi-Octave Voice is the Pandora's box that holds Aldous Huxley's images of the "antipodes of the mind," those images, emotions or sensations that don't belong to the utilitarian mind, as well as those of Antonin Artaud's *Theater of Cruelty* and Federico Garcia Lorca's **duende**. It is a voice that includes Jung's notion of the shadow and Goethe's words about Paganini playing the violin: "A mysterious power that all may feel, and no philosophy can explain." An Abraxian voice or a voice, as understood in the ancient Gnostic philosophical sources of knowledge, that reconciles and supports the presence of opposites. A voice that contains, as Noh theater creator Zeami described in his treatises, the "yugen" notion of the ineffable, profound, and mysterious beauty of the human experience.

If we think of expressionism as the art form accentuating the value of its representation by *intensifying* expression, I propose that my vision of the voice is fundamentally expressionist. Not only because of the life force released by the voice, but also because it reflects the intensely unfiltered substance of the person producing the sound. This potentially irrational expressionism of the voice forces both the doer (performer) and the viewer (audience) to invent new meanings and connections on and off the stage.

**Voice Made Visible**

I have often been asked, naturally so, why did I title my book *Voice Made Visible*? The voice is something perceptible, and though it is not my intention to get philosophical, there is a lot about it that simply touches into what is not visible, namable, or tangible.

As an actor before going on stage, I used to always remind myself of the etymology of the word "theater," which is "making visible that which is not." I have chosen to understand the voice also as a theater with a myriad of characters in it, as if one's voice was a **spelunker** opening uncharted trails in the secret subterranean cavities of our experience, our identities, and ourselves.

The idea of *visible* crystalized for me after reading Zeami's writings on the importance for the actor to operate with a "beginners mind."[3] Zeami encourages in his teachings that we as actors search our entire lives in hopes that one day, we see the voice and hear dance. This mystery has fed me, inspired me, and kept me busy through the years of my teaching and learning.

Visible, as in blatant, clear, and obvious, as when we are touched by someone's voice. When that happens, we are consumed and fully taken by their voice. In those moments something prodigious, inescapable, and absolute takes place.

That is why the singers we love are so important to us. Because there is something total, integral and fourth dimensional in the way we are affected by them. I can remember as a young man running to buy the latest LP release of my favorite band, The Beatles. Even though at the time I did not know it, that run was my way of galloping after the *unattainable*, the *absolute*... the voice of my favorite singer.

We can certainly express verbally our world of reality but how do we go about describing the realm of the absolute? That is where *"To see the voice... to hear dance"* must come in. Only through metaphors, allegories, and stories are we able to fully grasp theater. We may not be able to see the presence of the voice we hear, but our spirit certainly does. That is why it was so reassuring to "have" the recording in my hands. I was, at that very moment, one step closer to that which is unnamable.

I think of *visible* not so much as in something tangible, but as in something that is apparent, manifest, obvious, evident, discernible, and capable of being perceived. Visible is being seen, as much as a celestial body after an eclipse. **Eclipsing** our ego enables other voices to emerge.

*Voice Made Visible* relies fundamentally on four cornerstones of inspiration and each one of them is strongly anchored in traditional vocal practices:

**The Roy Hart Theatre:**
   for excavating the body, revealing hidden and raw sounds
**Spanish Cante Jondo:**
   for the depth and poignancy of its emotions
**Japanese Noh Theater:**
   for the representation of ghostly voices
**Shingon Shomio Chanting:**
   for the vocal imagination of their devotional practice

This book is a path to align the invisible connection that exists between the five inseparable components of one's voice: the breath, the body, the sound, the mind, and the spirit.

The Barrantes Voice System reveals the arsenal of sounds of the Multi-Octave Voice and its substance, grit, and authenticity. I strive to inspire the performer to make their *voice visible*.

**Notes**

1  This concept is explored more in *The Tuning of the World* by R. Murray Shafer (1981).
2  Etymologically from Greek *theatron*. "Theater" is a place for viewing where things are seen, revealed.
3  Zen Buddhist concept "shoshin" refers to the attitude of receptiveness, passion, and lack of bias while studying a subject.

# Chapter 3
# The Prerequisites
## Fiction and News

**Fiction**

*Figure 3.1* "Red Light/Green Light".

Having grown up as a Spaniard, I was very familiar with the physical and spiritual energy of *duende,* expressed in both flamenco and bullfighting, two of our cultural hallmarks. But it was only after my first visit to Japan in 1984 that I grasped the link between performers across borders and styles having this fundamental quality of being on stage.

French philosopher Simone Weil claimed that our imagination and **fiction** are at the core of our real life. What I call "Fiction" is something physical and perceptible and resides in the body. It is not a concept. It is a physical transformation that elevates one's state of being above the "daily" or "pedestrian body." It is an energetic, psychophysical, and psychosomatic understanding that is very present in Asian performing techniques, but not so much in the West.

Since Fiction is intimately connected to the body of the actor, the body of the actor needs to be "augmented," to become larger, hence "readable" for the stage. The moment we allow ourselves to slow our daily pace, much like in the game "Red Light/Green Light," then fiction will emerge offering us the possibility to unmask reality.

Fiction is the transformation that abandons the everyday realm. It is a heightened state of being in which skin, flesh and bones are reconnected to secure our theatrical metamorphosis. It is always good to remember that an audience is not looking at who you are, but rather at who you have become. It represents a fine line between the un-manifest and the manifest.

Our reality is quite often obscured; we use fiction to reveal our truths. Fiction consists of eclipsing oneself and one's **biography**. It changes the frame of reality. It means sacrificing one's body to embrace the incarnate body of the performer, the "other."

Though this ought to be a given for any actor on stage, since a part of you must cease to exist to become the other, as a theater professional, I often do not see this in practice in many performers and performances. As an audience, we should know "Fiction" is happening in the body, without being able to locate precisely *where* it is happening in the body on stage. We are talking of perception. If we are able to pinpoint it, then the performer is *telegraphing, ham acting, indicating,* or *showing* something rather than just *being it*. It is not exempt from bringing some discomfort, and I would suggest that a performer's body that has become too comfortable on stage has slipped back into the "daily."

Fiction is a vital element for the actor to make their voice visible. It is a shift of energy that takes place inside the body of the performer. Fiction is a subtle energy in the body of the performer that cannot be confused with the person performing it.

With Fiction, the body appears to be seething internally just like the innumerable bubbles clinging to the walls of a pot before it breaks into a boil. It is a "quality of being," a presence inherent not just to actors, but also dancers, singers, and even athletes.

A simple illustration that conveys the kinesthetic understanding of what I am describing is the suspension of action that occurs as the caller shouts the words "Red Light!" when playing the game "Red Light/Green Light." Everyone instantaneously suspends his or her actions. Fiction is that very instant, that "out of time" moment, that internally seething suspended state of being.

In the same way that we ask the audience to suspend their disbelief as they enter the theater, the performer must suspend their embodied reality to incarnate the "fiction" they are displaying for the audience. It is a matter of a non-visible yet perceptible extra effort in the body of the performer. Only in this unnatural and non-ordinary state of being created by Fiction, we as performers will be seen larger than life and be able to mislead the incredulity of the audience with our playing.

### *Actors and Athletes*

While teaching at Duke University, I had many young men and women in sports taking my classes. It was there that, after many conversations and hours of viewing their work, I began drawing connections between the actor and the athlete.

Our disciplines share a fundamental similar quality: we eclipse ourselves to change our daily habits in order to excel in the expression of our talent. Both the actor and the athlete must succeed under an extraordinary timeline of pressure and variety of circumstances. We strive to find the right gesture or action that encapsulates the most effective result to attain our goal. This goal is simply to engage the spectator, to captivate, and to suspend the audience's capacity for disbelief.

We gallop towards the place where we can trust our instincts to guide us; where our left hemisphere becomes available to instinct and our right hemisphere anticipates thinking. This pursuit leads us to the delicate dance that occurs between the individual, the self, the ego, the collective, and the group. We learn to make those moves concise, economic, and effective so they feed the character, the player, the team, and the ensemble. And in this, we draw from the best part of who we are: the self rather than the ego.

Both actors and athletes present a world to the public eye that looks natural, effortless, and as if magic is happening right then and there. In this presented world, the onlookers do not see the interminable hours of practice, rehearsals, failures, successes, and resilience built from the passion that drives the actor and the athlete to keep trying, growing, and mastering their craft.

The pillars of concentration, intensity, and focus we share are paramount to balance the distractions, obstacles, and external forces brought by the audience and/or the spectator. We learn to integrate them as they happen, making the athlete and performer fully available to adaptation in the present.

Freedom is gained by virtue of the training and the discipline that becomes integrated in the athlete and actor's bodies, making it appear natural, spontaneous, and real.

### Understanding Kinesthetically the Notion of Fiction Experiment

1) Lie down on the floor. Feel the weight of your head resting against it.
2) Now carefully lift your head just enough to allow a piece of paper to go between your head and the floor, no more than a millimeter or so.

That adjustment you just made is Fiction in your body.

### Tailor Position Experiment

Sit comfortably on the floor with your legs in **tailor position**. Allow all of your "**biographical**" idiosyncrasies to show up. Let the air come into you and with the next exhale begin to lengthen your spine, vertebrae by vertebrae. By the end of this action, you have attained Fiction in your body. Make sure you are not forcing or contracting your back in order to straighten it. Instead, simply allow your back to lengthen as if you had pneumatic bubbles between each vertebra.

*Figure 3.2* Sitting in tailor position.

### Sculptor and Clay Experiment

Two people are playing. One is the sculptor, the other is the sculpted. The task of the sculpted is to move from point A to point B at the far end of the room very slowly and on all fours without ever letting the knees touch the floor. The sculptor taps gently the back of the sculpted to indicate they can start moving in space. The sculpted then moves freely in slow motion across the space until the sculptor stops them by tapping their back again. The sculpted suspends their action in whatever position they find themselves in at that moment. This continues over the course of the journey from A to B. One tap releases the movement of the sculpted while the next tap makes them suspend their action. The sculptor wants to always take the sculpted by surprise, so they can never anticipate when they are going to be suspended in their movement. Every time the body of the sculpted is arrested that is Fiction! It is crucial that the sculpted does not hold their breath while maintaining their stillness and engaging their full body.

### Glass of Water Experiment

Start by carrying a half-full glass of water from one end of the room to the other. Assess how you felt executing this action. Now fill it up close to the rim and carry it to the opposite end of the room, without spilling one drop of it. Notice how your movement, breath, and body must adjust to this additional challenge, and how your focus is attuned as your daily body comes to life. That is Fiction.

*Figure 3.3* Glass of water imagery.

In her work, British novelist and Nobel Prize winner Doris Lessing implies that the moment we go inwardly into ourselves as human beings, we end up creating our own reality.

### *Hypo, Hyper and Tonic: The Three Muscular States*

There are three fundamentally distinct muscular states distinct muscular states of tonicity in your body. To experience them please lie down on your back resting your hands between your navel and pubis for this experiment.

A) ***Hypotonic***
   1) As you lie down facing up, touch your low abdomen with your hands. Notice that your low abdomen is floppy,

soft, and like Jell-O. This muscular state is what is called Hypotonic (less than Tonic).

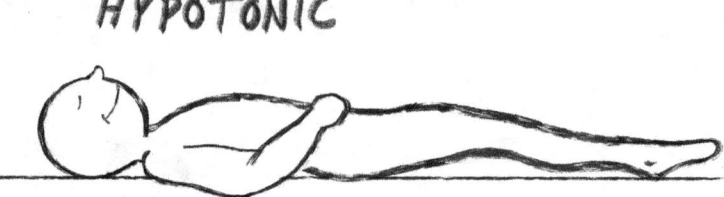

*Figure 3.4* Hypotonic position.

B) **Tonic**
1) This time you are going to simply bend your ankles at 90° and lift your head lightly up to look at them. Notice that your low abdomen is taut. This muscular state is **Tonic**. The desired optimal muscular state for Fiction.

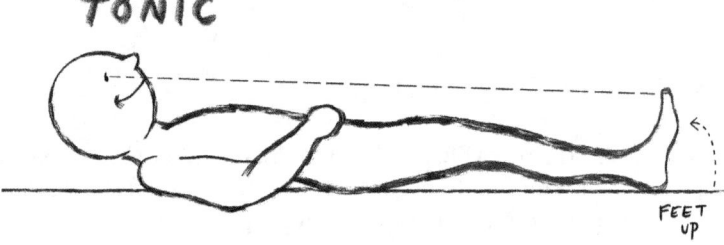

*Figure 3.5* Tonic position.

C) **Hypertonic**
1) This time you do the same as in "B" but keep lifting the head up. Notice this time that your low abdomen has contracted. This muscular state is called **Hypertonic** (more than Tonic). What happened is that the muscles went beyond the point of its own resistance becoming extra tight and consequently oxygen cannot reach the tissue.
2) A muscle that shakes or tremors is "calling" for oxygen.

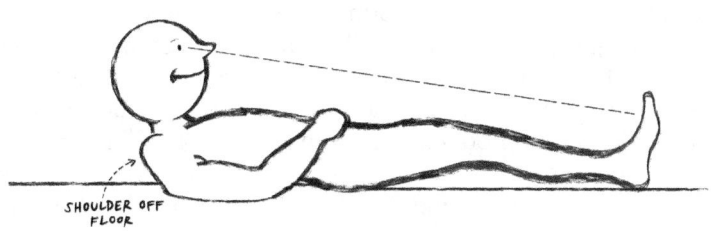

*Figure 3.6* Hypertonic position.

## News

*Figure 3.7* Newspaper.

*News is to the mind of the performer as FICTION is to the body.*

Since sound itself is invisible, the eyes become a key element in the chain of voice production and making the *voice visible*. I constantly request from my students and performers to "give me **News**," which is not so different from Stanislavski's idea "being in the moment" or Peter Brook's concept of the magic "*if.*" This issue is very simple. If you are in the business of telling stories, it is imperative that whatever you do on stage is "connected" to a specific image, emotion, sensation, perception, feeling, thought, or idea linked to what you are expressing. Performers are athletes of the soul, so they must make their gaze available, open, penetrable, and accessible to whatever the voice is expressing. News is that: an ephemeral, renewable, ever-present, constant flow of information (intellectual, sensorial, perceptual, experiential) that must be communicated.

Play, invent, and make things happen, but do not let the pupils of your eyes crystallize. If your imagination is out of focus, your eyes will betray you. The performer must absolutely avoid having the vacant gaze of a corpse, a talking head, or a zombie. No one enjoys watching the barren look of death, which is why we close the eyelids of the dead. A **crystallized** pupil is a crude reminder of a sterile and unproductive gaze that is the opposite of active, vibrant life.

Although it sounds simple, this in practice requires commitment. The performer must be willing to become "transparent" while unconditionally sharing the inner world they experience of the play. What this really means is that they must reveal themselves along with it, a technique that requires mastery. It is a marriage of the internal with the external.

Regarding "revealing," it is very important that all those potentially "uncomfortable garments" hung away in the closet (hate, longing, anger, love, compassion, tenderness, envy, desire, jealousy, etc.) must constantly be taken out of it and worn, confronted, unveiled repeatedly on stage.

*Figure 3.8* Laptop with news.

In the past eight years, I have seen thousands of actors in auditions. Time after time, the pupils of those performers were crystallized. They did not move, dilate, or contract. Their eyes were not alive. That paralyzed, immovable gaze of absence must be systematically revitalized. My simplest answer is to remind my students of the words the Duchess tells Alice in the Mock Turtle's story in *Alice in Wonderland*. The Duchess says Alice must take care of the sense and the sounds will follow[1].

The actor's voice must be in direct contact with the implicit emotional impulse that the voice carries. The task consists of how to direct the mind to the image, emotion, sensation, perception, feeling, thought, or idea and to naturally let the intention rise[2].

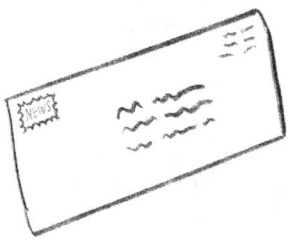

*Figure 3.9* Envelope delivering news.

*Connection* to what you are voicing is imperative, but so is the *desire* to communicate and express that connection. Without both these elements working simultaneously, your voice will not cooperate. This *sine qua non*[3] condition helps prevent voice work from devolving into a series of mechanical movements.

For example, consider singing a song. The whole mechanism of voice production is set in motion by your desire to communicate and serve that very song. It is that desire, along with your own personal connection to the material that results in News.

Singing a song without connection or without a real desire to communicate will simply be an empty, unrevealed voice. The bottom line is that the audience does not want to hear your voice; what they really want to hear is *you*.

There is a popular Spanish proverb that states, *"The eyes are the mirror of the soul."* What the performer expresses must be sharp, clear, never blurred. Another way to envision News is to think of your gaze while you are driving a car. In driving, you are constantly alternating between very specific and peripheral/general foci. You see the landscape but also the road signs, highway boards, the car on your right two lanes away, the one on your left passing you, and of course that one to the rear mirror approaching while you had time to look at your speed gauge and glance at the radio. And all that happens in milliseconds. You are alert, present, and connected. You are handling a machine that needs powerful control amongst other people doing the same thing. It is an unpredictable dance of the pupil of the eye, adjusting constantly to the reality of the moment. If you allow yourself to focus too long on one specific point while you drive, you run the risk of "zoning out," falling asleep, or having an accident. The same will happen to you on stage if you are disconnected and do not have News. The radical difference is that what you drive on stage is the powerful engine of the imagination.

Remember: the audience is demanding! We asked them for their time, money, and ability to suspend disbelief while sitting in their seat. If the story they are watching falls short of captivating their mind and spirit, they will fall asleep, think about tomorrow's shopping list, or worse, leave the theater.

When I speak of "News," I certainly think of newspapers, television channels or the web. News reaches the reader, and it holds our attention for a certain period. When that attention fades, we notice other headlines, scanning different sections until the eye settles on another set of news that compels us.

As an actor, when your connection to the material you are working on is fizzling out (and that is totally human), you do not need to be afraid of shifting over and over again to another "news channel." In daily life, this happens naturally and organically; yet, on the stage, it becomes a battle. Our discipline as performers is to fuel our work with a constant stream of News and seek its connection, because if you cannot connect with what you are saying or singing, why should the audience?

*Figure 3.10* Newsboy with newspaper.

For News, the mind of the performer should be porous, fertile, multiple. They should have plenty of mental room to shift, allowing agile, spontaneous changes in direction/image/thought while still fully committing to each one as it arrives. A quick-witted, permeable mind is like the flippers of a pinball machine trying to keep the ball alive and away from the drain, moving back and forth from an emotion to an image, or to a perception, or from an idea to a feeling, or a sensation . . . before your news stagnates or loses its vibrancy.

## Notes

1 Lewis Carroll's *Alice in Wonderland*. Published in 1970 by Flammarion, Paris.
2 Very similar to the notion of "News" is the concept of Apophenia, from the Greek *apo-* (away, off, apart) + *phainein* (to show). This term is used in the field of psychology to describe the perception of connections or meaning in unrelated or random phenomena.
3 A requirement; an absolute necessity.

## Chapter 4

# Sound Grounding

### The Eyes

A popular proverb tells us that *the eyes are the mirror of the soul.* The eyes are vital for voice production.

Moshé Feldenkrais,[1] author of *"Awareness through Movement,"* has found in his research that the softening of the muscles in and around your eyes has a very relevant effect on the softening of the muscles of your neck, and therefore on the muscles of your larynx.

In daily life, the connection between our eyes and our actions is done automatically, unless our own idiosyncrasies or neuroses come into play (i.e., not looking at the person with whom we are speaking, "spacing out," etc.).

On stage, this connection is not a given. It must be created.

### *Ideal Gaze Building*

As I have mentioned before, a "crystallized," "glazed," or "rigid" pupil is not something an actor can afford because it reminds us of the absence of life, which is death.

One of the ways to encourage an alive and dynamic gaze is to remind ourselves how we use our eyes when we drive a car. While driving, we fluctuate constantly between peripheral and selective or central vision; if we focus on one point for too long, we quickly become fatigued and drowsy and have a much higher chance of getting into an accident. This analogy can also be applied to the performer's crystalized eyes onstage.

The best way to avoid a crystalized pupil is to "GIVE NEWS!"

In other words, to engage yourself and the audience through the telling of your story with images, sensations, proprioception, feelings and emotions, thoughts, and ideas to feed simultaneously the story you are telling on stage. As a result, you have

DOI: 10.4324/9781003376842-5

a better chance of connecting to what you are saying. Your eyes will become engaged and engaging, which is the whole point of being a performer – to establish communication with the other.

## Ideal Gaze Building Experiment

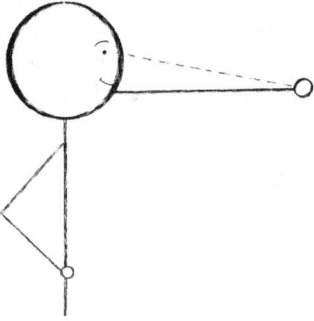

Figure 4.1 Proper neck position for ideal gaze building.

1) Stand in your **Relative Position** as if you were at sea level. Avoid any curving of the neck upwards (i.e., do not flamingo/guillotine neck) by gently combing your hair on the back of your neck/base of your skull upwards several times, lengthening your cervical belt, thus creating space between each vertebra.

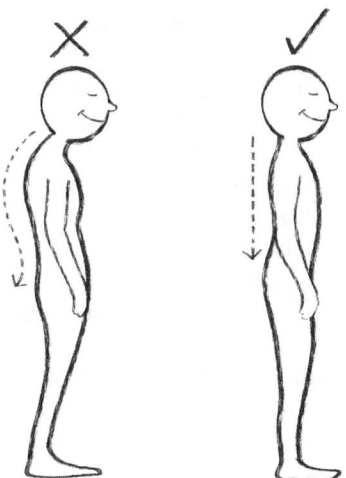

Figure 4.2. Proper spine lengthening for ideal gaze building.

2) Lengthen your whole spine by aligning the sternum and the navel on the same plane. Imagine you have a tiny emerald on your sternum emitting diamond fires. Your ears should be in line with the neck and shoulders.
3) Look straight ahead 10% below the horizon line, where sea and sky would meet if you were at the shore. Avoid creating a "double chin." Extend one arm forward with your thumb parallel to the horizon. Match the upper part of your thumb with the line of the horizon and direct your gaze to the lower part of your thumb.

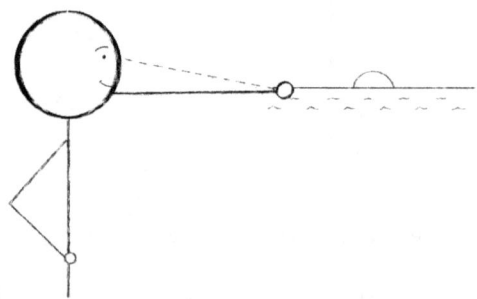

*Figure 4.3* For proper gaze, look straight ahead 10% below the horizon line.

### Consequence of this experiment

By aligning your gaze, your larynx got closer to your vertebral column, making the esophagus, which is attached to the diaphragm, descend into the thoracic cage thus creating more space for the larynx to go down. This makes the quality of your sound richer.

Freeing and lengthening the cervical belt allows the muscles and vertebral ligaments around them to open up and expand. These ligaments support the vertebrae in such a way that the vertebral column becomes a unified and compact vibrating instrument without hurdles in its way.

Coordinating your gaze with the lengthening of the spine contributes significantly to the **Acoustic Coupling** of the column of air and the column of sound, causing the most resonant and round vocal sound possible.[2]

### Imagery

- Visualize your head as a helium balloon attached by its string to the center of your abdomen (between the naval and pubis).

## Sound Grounding    31

Imagine this balloon swaying and floating lightly above your shoulders. Allow the lengthening of the head to pivot and oscillate in almost imperceptible micro movements all around the first cervical vertebrae (the "atlas") much like a buoy bobbing in a calm sea.

### *Trajectory of the Eyes Experiment*

You will be focused on the basic trajectories of the eyes during this experiment. To begin, do the following isolated eye movements in sets of four. If an uncomfortable, almost queasy feeling arises, stop, and focus on slow, **conditioned breathing**.

*Figure 4.4* Isolate your eye movements up and down. Repeat 4x.

RIGHT ————▷————▷— LEFT

*Figure 4.5* Isolate your eye movements right to left. Repeat 4x.

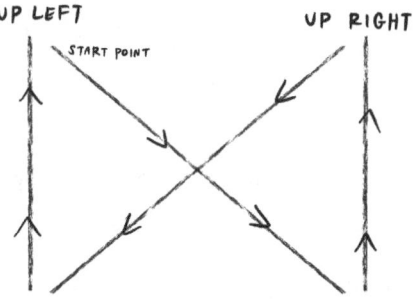

*Figure 4.6* Isolate your eye movements starting from up left, bottom right, up right, bottom left. Repeat 4x.

## 32  Sound Grounding

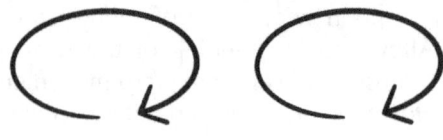

BASIC CIRCLES LEFT & RIGHT

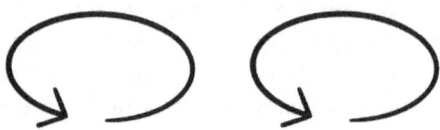

*Figure 4.7* Isolate your eye movements in basic circles. Repeat 4x to the right and 4x to the left. Avoid "exorcist" eyes . . . .

*Varying length foci*

10, 20, and 30 feet are the actual suggested distances.

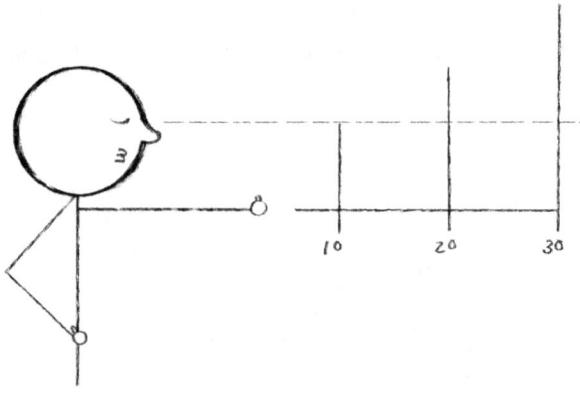

*Figure 4.8* Visual representation of various foci lengths.

## Head Resonators

Without delving too far into the scientific literature, for the purpose of this chapter we shall define resonation as the enhancement of a phonated sound. Consequently, we can state that sound can be improved and transformed by resonation.

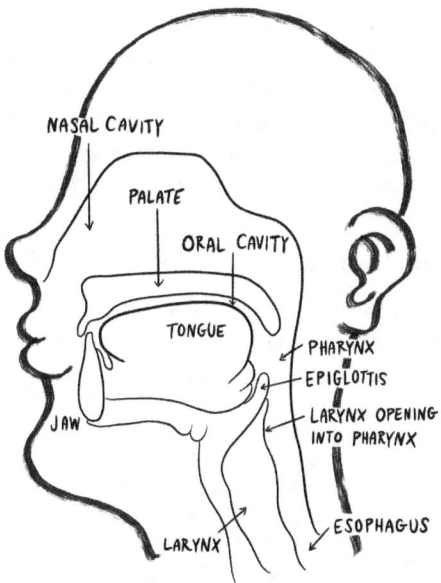

*Figure 4.9* Anatomy of the head for resonation.

### The Sinuses

The role of the sinuses in the Multi-Octave Range technique is very important particularly relative to adding **nasal quality** to sound, as well as enhancing Metal, Broken Metal, and Air **Voice Textures**.

The sinuses are a connected system of empty cavities within the skull and around the nasal cavity and the eyes. The sinuses help to lighten the weight of the bones in the head. They also help to warm and humidify incoming air. Apart from a thin layer of soft, pink tissue called mucosa, the sinuses are normally empty. The mucosa's secretions drain into three ridges of tissue in the nasal passage.

The human voice, much like a cello, a piano, or a guitar, has its own resonant chambers. As the sound vibrates and moves through those chambers, the sound acquires a certain color and texture.

The head has several resonators. From a purely acoustic point of view, the paranasal (around the nose area) sinuses are not technically resonators; however, from the proprioceptive point of view, they offer great assistance to the performer regarding quality, timbre, and placement of sound. Having clarified this point, I would like to include them under the 'head resonators,' in addition to the nasopharynx, oropharynx, and the laryngopharynx.

### The Four Paranasal Sinuses

Each sinus is named for the bone in which it is located. These are the different paranasal sinuses that you may be able to "feel" when you produce certain sounds that have a "metallic" quality:

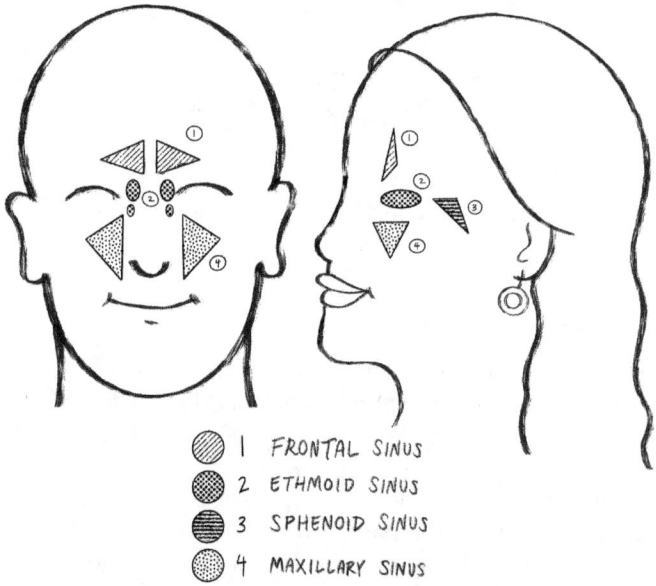

*Figure 4.10* Anatomy of the four paranasal sinuses.

**Frontal Sinus**: located in the low center of the forehead, above the orbital bone of each eye, within the frontal bone, behind the brow ridges.

**Ethmoid**: situated at the nasal bridge, its shape is cubical, and is relatively lightweight because of its spongy and honeycomb structure. It separates the nasal cavity from the brain and is located at the roof of the nose, between the two orbits.

**Sphenoid**: a bone behind the nasal cavity and the ethmoid sinuses. The body of the bone is basically cubical in shape and hollowed in its interior. Its shape suggests a bat or a butterfly with open wings.

**Maxillary Sinus:** the largest of the paranasal sinuses. It is located below the cheeks, above the teeth and on each side of the nose.

## The Mouth

There is no question the mouth is one of the important resonance chambers of the voice. The following experiments are designed to help you to experience the three basic types of mouth resonance I work on to optimize vocal production. I will be referring to proprioceptive notions, as well as placement, sound, vibration, and resonation.

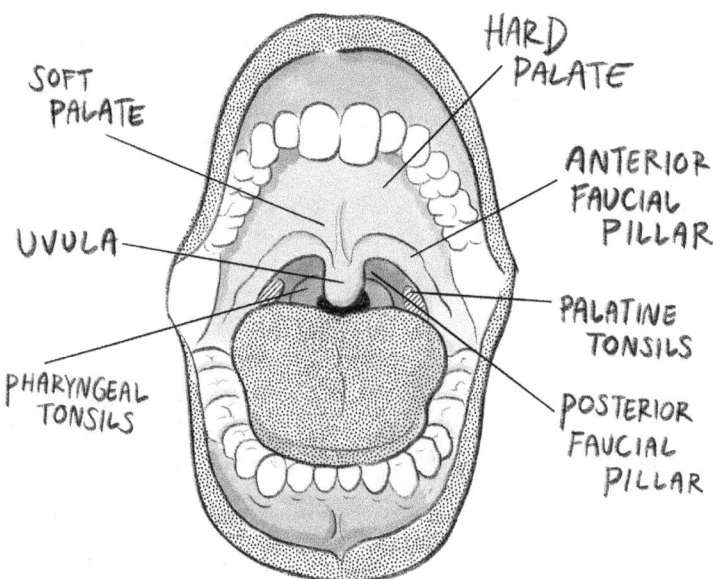

*Figure 4.11* Anatomy of the mouth.

### Proprioception of the Three Mouth Positions

**Mouth #1 with "N" in preparation for Tongue #1 or "Front Yard" Experiment**

Rest your top row of teeth on your bottom row without clenching your jaw. Your lips are resting on each other as well. Add a sustained "N" sound on your **Natural Pitch**. Your tongue is up against the upper ridge of your teeth. Notice how the front of your face from the forehead to your chin, "the mask," or what I often refer to as the "Front Yard," is activated with vibration. Feel the connection with your diaphragm as you make the sound.

**Mouth #2 with "M" in preparation for Tongue #2 or "Home" Experiment**

Your teeth now are no longer touching, but the lips still remain resting on each other. Allow 1/4-inch between your upper and lower teeth in a relaxed, dropped, and hanging loose Shower Mouth.

Add a sustained "M" sound on your Natural Pitch and be attentive to the difference in the feeling of the vibrations with the previous "Mouth 1." The tip of the tongue should rest behind the lower incisors.

Avoid tension. Feel the spherical nature of the space you are creating inside your mouth. Imagine the shape of a large plum or tangerine occupying this space.

Notice how the vibrations have now shifted and they are more centrally localized above and below your tongue.

**Mouth #3 with "NGA" in preparation for Tongue #3 or "Backyard" Experiment**

Start with the "M" sound as you did on the previous mouth position. On your Natural Pitch, gently initiate a slow-motion yawn shifting the sound from "M" to "NG" finishing by opening your lips with the sound of "NG-A."

Feel how the vibrations take place now between the soft palate and the nape of your neck. Your soft palate should be up (umbrella), and the back of the tongue has now dropped down (as in "Hot Potato") due to the yawn itself. Allow the mouth to drop and hang naturally as a result of the yawning action you induced.

To increase your proprioception, tap lightly on the nape of your neck until you feel a light tingling sensation in the area due to blood rushing to that area.

This experiment is fundamentally designed for you to understand sensorially and experientially the areas in which the three basic tongues are going to operate.

Notice how the sound resonates in the ensemble of your head as if you were wearing a motorbike helmet.

## The Pharynx

The pharynx is the membrane-lined cavity behind the nose and mouth, connecting them to the esophagus.

It extends from the base of the skull and the nose to the six cervical vertebrae. It acts like a tube, approximately five inches long and one inch wide, located in front of the cervical column. The pharynx is a part of both the digestive system and the respiratory system.

It is composed of three distinct areas: nasopharynx, oropharynx, and laryngopharynx.

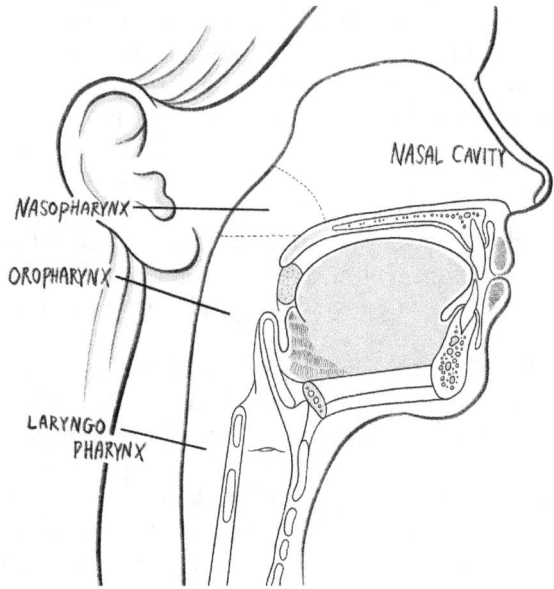

*Figure 4.12* Anatomy of the pharynx.

The pharynx is a powerful resonation chamber. The three pharyngeal cavities mentioned above are the primary resonation chambers for the voice. These three connecting cavities can be formed into many different shapes, each supporting or suppressing different overtone frequencies.

The pharyngeal constrictor muscles are a series of muscles that constrict in our throat when we swallow to make the food progress downwards through the esophagus towards the stomach. It is often the case that when we hear a tight, throaty voice, it means that these very muscles are being used (i.e., the sound we hear from a person that has a knot in their throat because they are "moved").

The pharynx is highly adjustable and can change its size and shape. This is the reason why the human voice has a greater range of expression than any other animal's voice or instrument.

Schematically speaking, anything to do with pure vocal sound production happens below the Adam's apple, whereas anything to do with the shaping of that vocal sound for speech and communication happens above the Adam's apple.

Regarding the resonant role of the pharynx, in daily life, vowels are easily and naturally shaped in the oral cavity; however, for the stage, it is far more efficient to shape them further back using the ensemble of the pharynx. The resonance for the stage will be fuller and stronger if resonated in the pharynx, freeing up the oral cavity, tongue, and lips to articulate the consonants.

### A Note about Tension

If the breathing muscles are tensed, the muscular tissues that surround the larynx will also become tensed. This tension will diminish the ability of the voice to be able to respond directly to brain stimulus.

If the subtle muscles of the larynx become tensed, unfortunately they cannot be applied to the needs of a given Voice Texture.

These are the three typical areas of tension to be aware of:

1) Tension on the upper area of the larynx and thoracic girth when high, light, and stridently pitched sounds are produced.
2) Tension at the low area of the larynx, like in very deep male voices with a "basso profundo" quality.

3) Nasal tension when the soft palate and the back of the tongue get too close to each other.

Now let us take a closer look at each of the three distinct areas of the pharynx.

### I. Nasopharynx

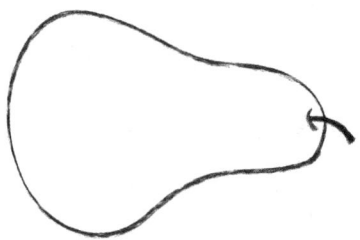

Figure 4.13 A pear representing the nasopharynx.

As its name indicates, this area is at the very back of the nose. This is the area you feel when you overdo the intake of wasabi with your sushi...

Of all the head resonators, only the nasopharynx can change its size due to the extraordinary mobility of the soft palate. This translates to offering a large variety of vocal qualities.

The optimal conditions for nasal cavity resonation are somewhat paradoxically created by the ability to produce subtle adjustments in the oropharynx, which starts at the soft palate (see following section on "Oropharynx").

### II. The Oropharynx

This area includes the very back of the tongue, the soft palate, the sidewalls of the throat, the arches of the palate, the tonsils, and the pharyngeal constrictor muscles. The soft palate plays the lead role in the process of phonation; its position influences significantly the resonance of the oropharyngeal channel and intervenes strongly in the color properties of sound. Vocal quality depends a great deal on the degree of the soft-palate muscular activity. For these reasons, the soft palate should be constantly active while singing. A sagittal view of this area could be represented in its shape by a tangerine. This is also the area where you feel sensation when eating ginger.

*Figure 4.14* A tangerine representing the oropharynx.

In its usual position, the soft palate hangs into the pharyngeal cavity with what is known as the uvula, which is a fleshy suspended appendage like the clapper of a bell. The soft palate and especially the uvula are richly innervated and affect the muscle tone throughout the larynx. The uvula secretes saliva to moisten and keep our throats lubricated, as well as to prevent food and fluids from going into the nose. This area, in combination with the pharyngeal constrictor muscles, is strongly recruited when producing Air sounds.

The oropharynx is located behind the oral cavity and extends from the uvula to the level of the hyoid bone, which is a horseshoe-like bone below your mandible and between your chin and the thyroid cartilage. This bone serves as the base for the tongue. Its peculiarity as a bone is that it is the only bone in the body that does not articulate in conjunction with another bone, so it is in a sense "suspended." It can easily be palpated and even gently massaged.

The oropharynx is directly affected by various anatomical elements surrounding it, such as the pharyngeal constrictor muscles, the tongue, and the jaw.

### *Pharyngeal Constrictor Muscles*

The pharyngeal constrictor muscles are a group of muscles in three layers:

- *Superior*, back and behind the mouth.
- *Medium*, in between the superior and the inferior.

- *Inferior*, behind the larynx extending downwards towards the trachea.

Their main function is to sequentially move whatever we ingest from the pharynx into the esophagus. They contract reflexively and successively from top to bottom when we swallow food or liquids. They work in synergy with the muscles that elevate the larynx. Schematically, we can say that all "upward" laryngeal movement is accompanied by a tightening of the pharynx, while all "downward" movement is associated with a relaxation of the pharyngeal constrictor muscles.

The pharyngeal constrictor muscles, even though they are not a sphincter muscle, act like one. They can vary the diameter of the pharyngeal tube in the same way that the diaphragm lengthens the pharyngeal tube when it contracts and descends into the low abdomen, thus improving voice production. These muscles can contribute considerably to augment and improve the resonance of low harmonics.

Relaxing these muscles:

- **Yawning**: Most voice schools agree that yawning is the best and most natural thing to do to soften tension and relax one's vocal muscles.
- **Sniffing**: Encourage breathing in gently and deeply (encouraging low abdominal breathing) as if perceiving a very valuable and delicate scent; maintain the feeling of a dome behind the nose and allow the sides of your nostrils to flare slightly. Maintain this feeling when producing sound.
- **Ruminating**: With your mouth closed, produce the "M" sound mimicking gently with your jaw the lateral, vertical, and circular small ruminating motions that cows do when feeding on grass and chewing their cud.

### Tongue

The tongue for the performer is a vital muscle when we produce vocal sound, as well as when we articulate our speech and use our diction.

To ease this strong and complex muscle and to get the maximum number of hurdles out of its way when you unravel the Five

Voice Textures in this book, please refer to "**Shower Mouth**" and "Three Tongues" in Chapter 5.

To strengthen and master your practice, I very strongly recommend that you marry the Barrantes Voice System with the necessary demands that diction and speech require, since both skills are complementary to each other.

### *The Jaw*

The mandible, or inferior maxillary bone, forms the lower jaw with its characteristically curved horseshoe-like shape. It is a very relevant bone in voice production because of the role it has in determining the size of the oropharynx and the aperture of the mouth. It connects with the skull (the temporal bones) via the temporomandibular joint (TMJ).

It is important to bring awareness to this area in our body given the number of students that constantly arrive in class distressed by the discomfort and severe pain they often experience in this particular area of their mouth.

The mandible interacts with the skull via the temporalis muscle and with the masseter muscle below our cheeks that brings the teeth together for mastication. When you clench your teeth, you feel the masseter muscle (on your cheek) and the temporalis muscle (on the side of your forehead). Over-extending this joint will make your jaw "pop" with a sound (avoid popping your jaw gratuitously). The opening of your mouth beyond this "popping point" can produce a painful locking of the jaw ("lockjaw"). An unaligned bite of the teeth or clenching of them for an extended period (i.e., teeth grinding at night) can cause migraines and intense chronic headaches.

Because the joint acts like a hinge with a sliding and translating motion, it makes this joint a very complicated one and prone to malfunction. A considerable number of people suffer from Temporo-Mandibular-Joint or TMJ Syndrome.

For more complementary considerations and experiments on this area of your body, please refer to "Shower Mouth" in Chapter 5.

### *Ways of Relaxing Your Jaw*

To counteract the tensions that can build up in the jaw and its associated muscles from daily use, we must mindfully work to release and relax the jaw.

## Relaxing Your Lower Jaw

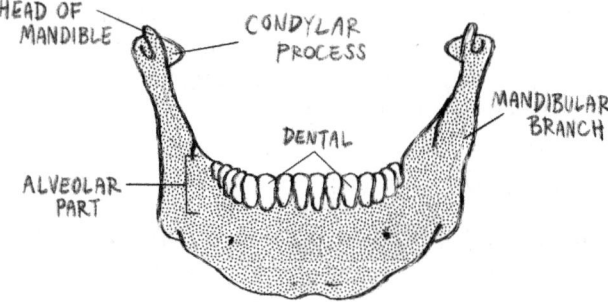

*Figure 4.15* Anatomy of the lower jaw.

1) Take an open second position with your body. Bend your knees so your torso is settled. Lengthen your spine. Arms at an inverted 10:10 position (see page 146). Bring your palms together without changing your elbow–shoulder relationship. Your armpits should be opened. Imagine letting the air permeate your armpits as if allowing many hazelnuts that you were holding in your pits to fall and scatter on the floor.
2) Use Shower Mouth (see page 98). Shake your hands at the height of your sternum releasing a long "NGA." Hear the natural oscillation of the sound, which should be loose.

The French use often in daily life the expression of "being on a B mouth" – "être bouche bée" – which translates roughly to "agape" because of the way your mouth relaxes open completely after releasing the phonation of a "B" sound. Simply put, it means to be absolutely surprised, flabbergasted, stunned, relaxed and open-mouthed.

*Figure 4.16* Edvard Munch's *The Scream* illustrates a dropped lower jaw.

Remember: make sure that the jaw shakes but not the head. Avoid whiplashing. The cervical belt is lengthened. Several voice schools encourage grabbing the chin with one hand to shake the jaw. I have seen this violent approach often and I am inclined to avoid it. Employing force is like war: it might be something inevitable, but it is never useful.

*Massaging Your TMJ and SCM*

This is a very soft, yet efficient tissue manipulation. The whole point of this approach is to loosen the fascia[3] of your muscles related to your jaw: both your TMJ as well as your SCM (sternocleidomastoid muscle), which joins your head to your clavicle. The SCM is the first muscle, closest to your jaw, that you can feel when you turn your head to one side.

### Massaging Your TMJ and SCM Experiment

1) Starting from the clavicle, apply light upwards pressure very gently but constantly, like the pressure we apply when we try to feel the pulse in our wrist. Allow the fascia overlaying the muscles to elongate slowly. You should do this slowly over four to five minutes.
2) Your gentle touch, with three/four of your fingers or your knuckles, should carry the skin tissue along with you as you move up towards your scalp. Avoid having a deep pressing or rubbing motion as you do this and avoid sinking into your temples. Simply go up toward your skull, gently scooping the myofascial tissue through your skin. We are lightly elongating *upward* toward your temples and even above the hairline, but not *downward*.

### Masseter Experiment

1) Now do the same starting at the bottom of the masseter going up. Use three/four fingers or even your knuckles to give you a broader surface. No more than 3 to 4 lbs. of light pressure as in the previous experiment. You might feel it on your neck because of the interconnectedness of tissue. You will most likely feel your jaw afterwards, like a heavy dropped curtain, with a tingling sensation.

End up by delineating/caressing/massaging the masseter with a very gentle downwards slow motion.

## Imagery

- Shower Mouth.
- Edvard Munch's painting *The Scream*.
- Horse, hippopotamus, crocodile, snake.
- "Bouche bée".

## III: The Laryngopharynx

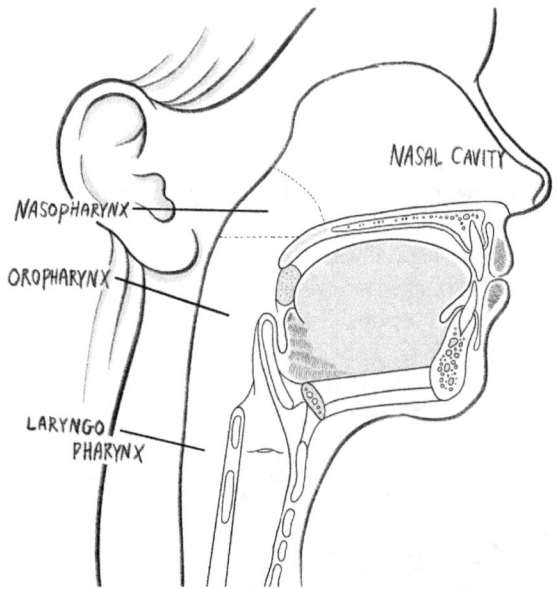

*Figure 4.17* Anatomy of the laryngopharynx.

The laryngopharynx is that area in the body between the hyoid bone, where it attaches, and the esophagus. It extends from the epiglottis to the inferior border of the cricoid cartilage. It corresponds basically to the vertebral area C3–C6. Both air and food pass through it. The laryngopharynx is often referred to as the "voice box." Its upper part connects with the pharynx, the lower part with the trachea. On the front, it is just below the skin, and behind it we find the esophagus. It is involved in sound production (volume and **pitch**), breathing, and swallowing. It looks like a short pipe and includes several cartilages: the epiglottis,[4] thyroid, **arytenoid**, and **cricoid**, as well as a complex network of ligaments. It moves vertically and in conjunction with the trachea.

A sagittal view of this area could suggest a kiwi in shape. In terms of inner proprioception, this is the area you feel stimulated when you drink a smooth whiskey.

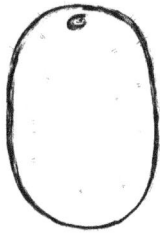

*Figure 4.18* A kiwi representing the laryngopharynx.

When we breathe without making sound, the vocal cords are fully open at the back. They relax by the larynx walls, leaving the glottal passage fully open.

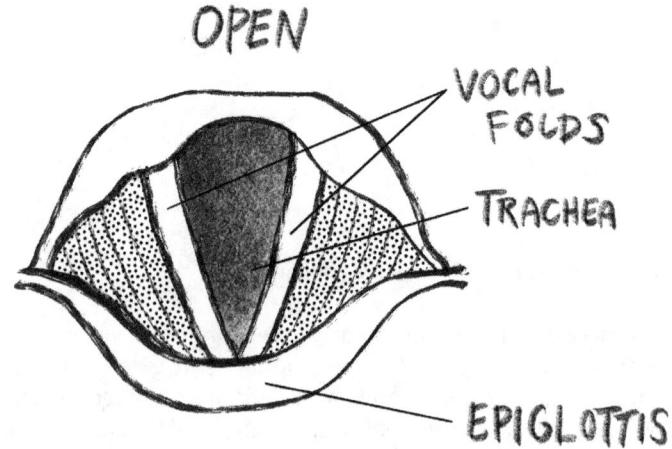

*Figure 4.19* Fully open vocal cords, the trachea, and the epiglottis.

When we speak, the vocal cords, which are stretched across the glottal passage, vibrate due to the air that is being released from the lungs, thus producing sound.

The higher the pitch, the vocal cords become thinner and tighter. The lower the pitch, the vocal cords are thicker and more relaxed.

Remember that anything related to voice production of sound, like voice textures and intensity, is controlled by the larynx, while anything to do with voice and speech, such as diction and pronunciation,[5] are determined using the palate, tongue, teeth, and lips.

Schematically speaking, one can say that all upward laryngeal movement is always accompanied by the larynx becoming tighter and smaller. The constrictor pharyngeal muscles work in synergy with the elevator muscles of the larynx. You will clearly notice this when you do a vocal run going up from your Natural Pitch to the highest comfortable note you can produce. The same occurs when we produce Air sounds.

The opposite is also true: when the larynx descends, the glottal passage is enlarged, and a relaxation of the constrictor pharyngeal muscles takes place. The larynx can be lowered down by a group of muscles situated below the hyoid bone or by the diaphragm (i.e., when you yawn, the larynx descends).

## Larynx Experiment

1) Place your fingers on your Adam's apple and simply notice what happens as you do the vocalizations I mentioned earlier:

- A vocal run up.
- A vocal run down.
- Yawning.

## The Thyroid Cartilage

The thyroid[6] is the most voluminous of the larynx cartilages. Its shape suggests an open book with its spine being visible to the viewer, below the Adam's apple. The two sides of this cartilage cover the sides of the trachea much like a shield. It protects and supports the vocal folds, which are lodged behind it. Movement of this cartilage can produce tension in the vocal folds and subsequently modify voice quality. One can palpate it and move it side to side easily (but do so very gently) because it is right behind the skin where the Adam's apple is located.

The Adam's apple is more prominent and visible in men due to natural male hormonal development at puberty, making the folds thicker and shorter.

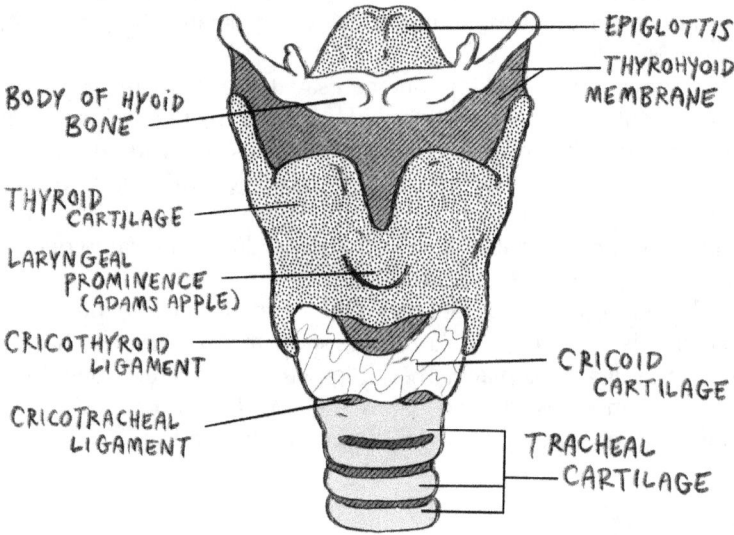

*Figure 4.20* Anatomy of the thyroid cartilage.

### The Vocal Folds

The vocal folds, or vocal cords, are two strong elastic mucous membranes stretched horizontally above the trachea. They vibrate to produce sound for speaking and singing. Even though there could be many factors determining the outcome for our individual voice pitch, we can generally say that the male voice is deeper in pitch due to the thickness and length of the vocal cords. In male puberty, the vocal folds might even double in length, causing the change of voice into a significantly deeper tone. The vocal folds are part of the glottis[7] area. When we inhale and exhale, the glottis remains immovably open.

The vocal folds share three movements:

- Wide open when we inhale.
- Closed when we are in apnea.[8]
- Vibrating in phonation.

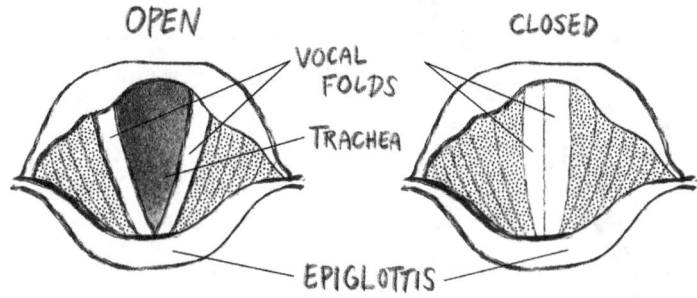

*Figure 4.21* Opened vocal folds vs. closed vocal folds.

The vocal folds function like the reeds of a wind instrument. The air pressure going through them makes them open and vibrates as we exhale. For them to vibrate, it is imperative that they touch. However, to avoid damage due to their constant vibration in phonation, the vocal folds are lubricated by mucosa (epithelium), which is what is making contact during phonation. When we sing, the vocal folds open and close at the amazing rate of 440 times per second. Pitch, intensity, and timbre (tone quality) of a sound depend on the subglottic (below the glottis) pressure.

The vocal folds lengthen when we produce high sounds. They are shorter on the lower notes, just like a rubber band that is being pulled, or a guitar string being tuned. The folds' color is white because they have little blood circulation. The epithelium, or elastic mucosa, covering the folds is like skin and it contributes to the proper vibration of the vocal folds.

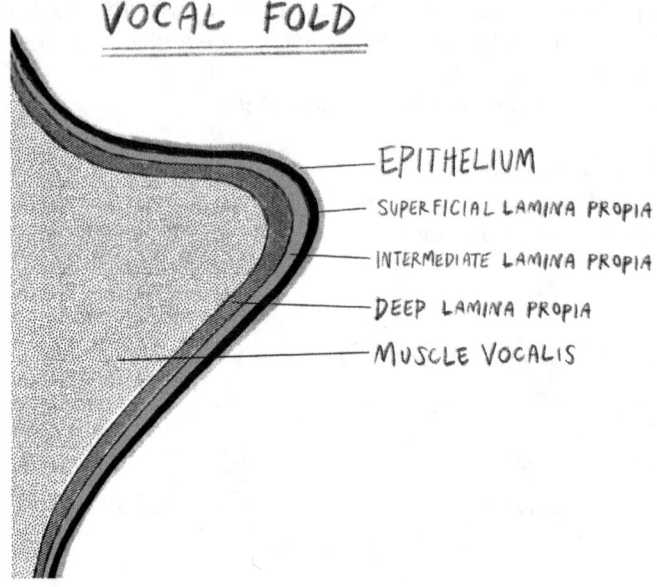

*Figure 4.22* Cross-section of the vocal fold.

This layer can get undesirably thicker by simple use, like fatigue or even age. Yet it can thicken excessively with heavy use and/or abuse, such as yelling in concerts or sporting events, to the point of creating unfortunate pathologies like laryngitis (swelling of the vocal cords), nodules (localized thickening of the fold), cysts (a tiny pouch-like gathering fluid), or polyps (soft, tiny lump formed by blood and blood vessels).

Swelling of the vocal folds makes them vibrate unevenly, resulting in hoarseness and strained breathiness.

Causes for hoarseness can be viral infections, abuse of the voice, allergies, acid reflux, smoking, or psychological.

### The Ventricular Bands

The ventricular bands, or vestibular folds, are also commonly called the "false vocal cords." They are situated parallel and above the vocal folds. They are composed of a mucous membrane with ligaments that have a moisturizing and protective role. In phonation, they participate in sounds like: Broken Earth "Cookie Monster" voice, Water sounds, coughing, deep "death metal" rock voices, etc. They play a protective role for the vocal cords providing moisture and lubrication.

The ventricular bands affect phonation and the quality of sound. The sounds of Tibetan chanting and Tuvan throat singing imply the use of both the vocal folds, as well as the ventricular bands. Done properly and with support of the diaphragm, these sounds, though not necessarily easy to control, should not harm the performer.

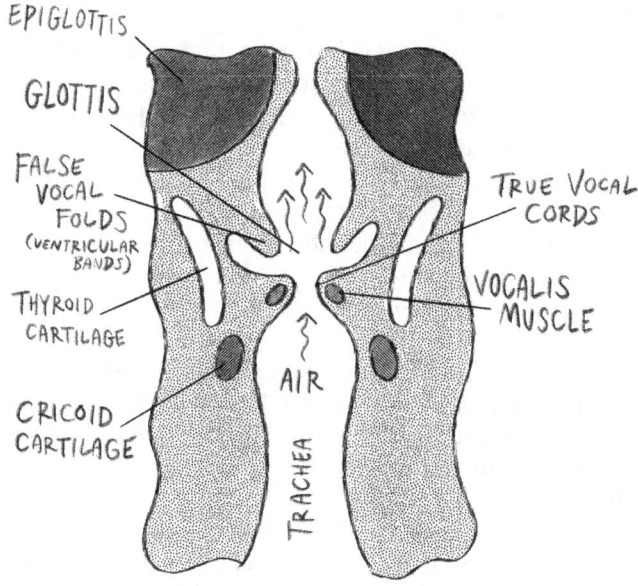

*Figure 4.23*  Air flowing through the glottal and ventricular bands areas.


### The Thorax

The torso stabilizes our spine, connecting us to our limbs and the pelvis. The most critical organs of the body are contained within it. The diaphragm separates the upper part of the torso, the thorax, from the lower part, the abdomen.

### *Spine Alignment*

Spine alignment is essential to produce sound safely and efficiently. When the spine is properly aligned in Relative Position, the muscles associated with the diaphragm attain their optimum relaxing length. This helps our ability to manage muscular vocal power, pitch, and pace for the stage. Regarding our vocal muscularity, we can say that our ability to control our breath is more important than how much breath capacity we have.

In addition to the groundbreaking studies and practice revealed by the Alexander Technique, I would like to mention the important contributions of the French neurophysiologist and phoniatrician, Dr. Alfred A. Tomatis.

Dr. Tomatis was interested in how sound is transmitted both through air and bone vibration. He believed that a well-balanced vibrating larynx should go together with the bone's ability to transmit and resonate the voice.

Alignment of the spine produces muscular tonicity, which is necessary to foster bone vibration. Healthy vocal production works best when it combines the work of the larynx and the breathing system with ease.

There are two reasons for this:

1) The area of the larynx closer to the spine moves nearer to the cervical vertebrae, while the esophagus, which is attached to the diaphragm, moves down causing the lengthening of the dorsal spinal curve. Together, this action creates a freer, clearer pathway for vocal sound production.
2) Thanks to this alignment, the spine's muscles and ligaments work together, creating a single compact column of air and sound that vibrates freely due to the vibrations produced by the larynx. I often refer to this phenomenon as acoustic coupling of the voice.

### The Cervical Belt

The area connecting the head and torso is important in that it has a strong musculature but is also quite flexible.

We should pay particular attention to three areas:

1) The top of the neck (C1 and C2) known as the "atlas" and "axis" vertebrae, respectively, for their mobility.
2) The middle of the neck (C4) because of its curvature.

3) The bottom cervical vertebra (C7) being the bridge between the head and torso.

For all the exercises concerning the cervical belt, I very strongly recommend the image of always maintaining a pneumatic bubble (like the ones in a spirit level tool) between each vertebra. This image aids in releasing compression between the vertebrae, helping to lengthen this area.

If in doubt, whenever you take or tilt your head back, be sure to support the neck with one hand as you do it, and certainly never push or pull the head down. The relationship between the neck and the top of your skull should be like that of a dome on a strong foundation, the shoulders.

### Yes/No Experiment

Stand in your Relative Position. Eight counts for your head nodding "yes" lightly and then eight counts for your head shaking "no" lightly, lengthening your cervical belt, never allowing your vertebrae to compress. Visualize pneumatic air bubbles in between each vertebra.

### Axes Experiment

Stand in Relative Position. Fully lengthen your spine. Eight counts for your head turning right and eight counts for your head turning left. Then eight counts for your head going down (chin to chest) and eight counts for your head coming back to starting position.

### Circles Experiment

Stand in Relative Position. Four counts for your head circling to the right, up, slightly back, around, chin to chest, and then four counts to the left. Make sure that while you gently circle your head around you never compress your vertebrae. Lift your cervical belt up and back, either imagining you were placing your fist behind it and wanted to stretch the neck up and over it, or in fact placing your hand on the back of your neck to physically encourage that lengthening/lifting.

### Cloud Viewing Experiment

Stand in Relative Position with your gaze straight ahead.

Center cloud viewing:

1) Eight counts to gradually lift the gaze (and head) up 45°, always avoiding the slightest compression of your cervical belt.
2) Eight counts to stay in that position as if looking at the clouds in the sky at a 45° angle, but never straight above you. Straight above would be a 90° angle and would almost certainly force compression of the cervical vertebrae.
3) Eight counts to come down to where you began.

Right side cloud viewing:

Starting with your head in the center with gaze straight ahead, take eight counts to move the head to the right side then repeat the same sequence of 24 counts (up to the right, stay there, down to the right).

Left side cloud viewing:

Eight counts to move to the left side, then repeat the sequence of 24 counts.

### Listening to Your Shoulder Experiment

Stand in your Relative Position. Keeping your face forward, tilt your head, up and over, with your right ear towards your right shoulder, never squashing your vertebrae. Aim your left ear up towards the ceiling, as if you were listening to someone on the floor above you. Do not raise your shoulder to meet your ear – allow there to be natural space between them. Then do the other side. Repeat twice on each side.

### Pigeon's Neck Experiment

Stand in Relative Position. Encourage soft mobility of your head forward and back, focusing on the middle and low cervical areas. Avoid at all costs creating a double chin. Keep your cervical belt airy and lengthened.

## Frontal Stretch Experiment

Stand in Relative Position. Spine fully lengthened. Interlace your fingers behind your back at the level of your waistline. On eight counts, stretch the arms down towards the floor, so they end up by the midline of your gluteus. Hold that position for eight counts, and then release the clasp of the hands. Rest for eight counts and repeat again.

## Cornerstones

- Always encourage the lengthening of your cervical belt as if you were combing your hair and cervical belt upwards.
- Establish the awareness of your sternum as if you had a tiny, glistening emerald shining there.
- Always avoid a double chin when you lengthen your cervical belt.

## Imagery

- Frankenstein's neck bolt being unscrewed. The sides of the neck moving gently towards the shoulders, ending up with the broadest neck ever.
- If you ever have worn a Renaissance costume with ruffle around your neck, imagine your neck finishing where the perimeter of the prop does. You should feel your glottal area broadening.

## The Solar Plexus

The solar plexus is a web of incoming and outgoing radiating nerve fibers. It is located in the upper part of the abdomen just below the sternum and behind the stomach. According to Hindu tradition, the solar plexus is the third chakra and deals with metabolism, digestion, raw emotions, self-esteem, self-discipline, and intuition. It also regulates numerous vital functions like heart rate, digestion, respiratory rate, pupillary response, urination, defecation, and sexual arousal. Common sensations associated with this neuralgic center are anxiety, shortness of breath, or as a "knot in the stomach."

Expressing certain sounds with proper abdominal breathing support helps us to relax the solar plexus. This can create both a sensation of relief but also vulnerability, feelings of anxiety, or even nausea. When managed correctly, however, this can be considered a sign of cleansing, thus reestablishing the energetic power of the voice. This is a very important element to factor in voice training because we are not only wanting to attain technical proficiency, but also an expressive voice that is emotionally connected to our inner worlds.

### Ribs as Gills

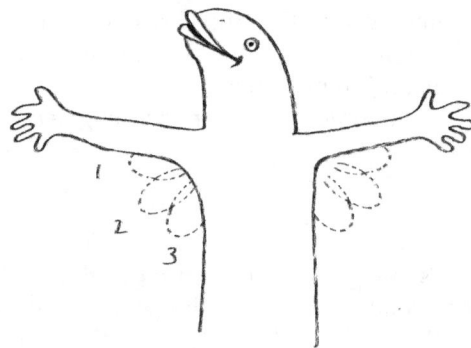

*Figure 4.24* Imagine you have gills on your ribs for breathing.

The intercostal muscles, in combination with our ribs and the diaphragm, assist us with breathing. I refer to the ribs imaginatively as the "gills" because this image helps us to visualize the lateral motion of our rib cage, which for our stagecraft is most productive. Why? Because envisioning these muscles in this way encourages the expansion of the diaphragm as a 360° dome or parachute, instead of the more common way breathing is thought of, which is primarily through the chest moving up, down, and forward.

The intercostal muscles are situated between the ribs in three layers:

1) Eleven external intercostal muscles are on either side of the ribs. They raise the ribs and expand the chest cavity during inhalation. They also assist in forced and quiet inhalation.

2) Eleven internal intercostal muscles are on either side of the ribs. When these muscles contract, the ribs are lowered and the thorax contracts to assist with exhalation.
3) The third layer, made up of the innermost intercostal muscles, is the deepest of the three intercostal layers. It also assists in exhalation.

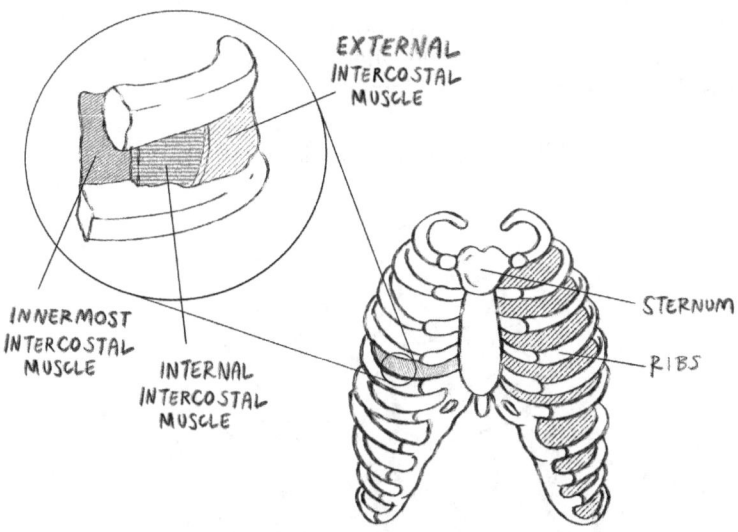

*Figure 4.25* Anatomy of the intercostal muscles.

There is another important set of muscles, the elevator muscles of the ribs, which are located at the back of the thoracic cage. These are small, deep, and numerous, and they help to elevate the ribs for deep inspiration. These muscles help "put on the brakes" during exhaling, thus controlling the amount of breath in the **subglottal area**. They also help to reestablish proper posture for people who tend to lean forward while producing sound. If you flex your upper torso forward or up, especially when laying down facing up, you can easily feel these muscles.

### The Diaphragm ("The Power Tool")

In all voice techniques, we often hear the expression "support the sound! . . . use your diaphragm!" . . . so let us talk about it.

Since antiquity, the diaphragm has been considered the primary muscle for breathing. Its contraction at birth forces us to bring the first scream into life. We use it relentlessly until we take our last breath, and its function can be both automatic and voluntary. Of course, the diaphragm plays an important role in breathing, but it is also essential for vomiting, urinating, and defecating.

Daily breathing is a reflexive act controlled by the autonomic sympathetic nervous system. However, this system can also be controlled, as we can decide when and how to breathe. This is an essential aspect for vocal training.

The diaphragm muscle is shaped like an asymmetrical dome that separates the thorax from the abdomen.

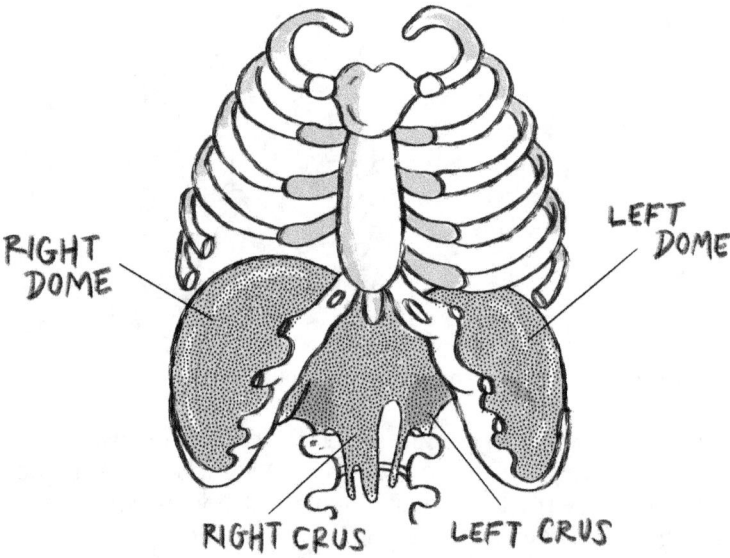

*Figure 4.26* Anatomy of the diaphragm.

The diaphragm is composed of two areas. The first, the central tendon, is a sheath of flat, broad muscle fibers that can expand sideways, much like a parachute or an umbrella. The second area is formed by concentric fibers that can contract and radiate around the thoracic cage. When the diaphragm contracts, it pushes the esophagus, the trachea, and the larynx back to their original locations in the body.

Sound Grounding 59

As we know, the diaphragm can be considered an involuntary muscle. But it can also be voluntarily activated when we take a deliberate inhalation to get more air. Indeed, training this muscle is essential for the range of needs a voice requires on the stage. An actor who does not use the diaphragm correctly risks stress, undesirable effort, and potential vocal pathologies that can hurt and even permanently damage the vocal instrument.

### *Inspiration*

The diaphragm can move in two different ways:

1) Like a Piston:

Pressure in the lungs decreases and air rushes in. The diaphragm contracts and the central tendon descends, much like a piston, bringing along the lungs downwards into the torso. This action increases the air volume in the lungs which become wider all around and make the rib cage expand slightly upwards and outwards. This is exactly why we want to train this muscle for the stage: to increase and control its intake and output of air. The abdominal viscera are pushed downward by the pressure, giving the appearance of what I often refer to in class as "**Buddha Belly**" or "**Inner Tube**."

*Figure 4.27* Buddha Belly illustrating the abdomen expanding.

2) Like the Gills of a Fish or a Broad Parachute:

Pressure in the lungs decreases and air rushes in. The descent of the central tendon is contained by the abdomen, which creates an almost flat "wall" that follows the same vertical plane of the sternum. This "wall" should never be created through muscular contraction or by being pulled or sucked into the abdomen. The pressure created by the diaphragm causes the ribs (*gills*) to rise from within the thoracic cage, thus enlarging its diameter. In this scenario, the diaphragm moves outwards from the fixed center of the central tendon. The sides of your torso move outwards too, much like the gills of a large fish, or a parachute or umbrella that opens fully. This way of inhaling is most practical and available for dancers, since they need to protect their abdominal organs by tonifying/flattening, but not tucking in, their abdominal "wall."

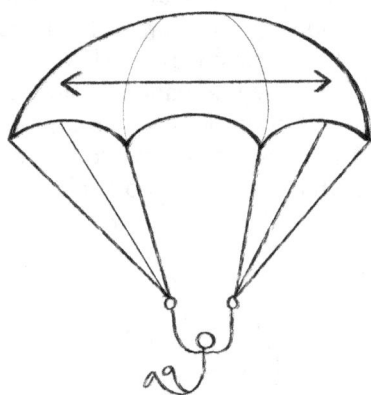

*Figure 4.28* Expand your upper torso like a fully open parachute.

### *Expiration*

When pressure in the lungs increases, air of course is pushed out. And when the diaphragm and intercostal muscles relax, the diaphragm assumes its dome-shaped structure while the ribcage naturally descends.

The training of the diaphragm for the stage consists in making sure that the exit of the exhaled air is tempered, reigned in, and "dosed" accordingly.

In a way, it is as if we are "putting the brakes on" the exhaling muscles. The torso can do this either by maintaining a "Buddha Belly/Inner Tube" or by using the "gills approach" (the intercostal muscles) while exhaling.

The cooperation between the diaphragm and the larynx is very important to satisfy the needs of our voices on the stage. How to control one's breath depends on the amount of airflow needed in the larynx. For the larynx to vibrate properly, one must never use excessive force.

The same applies for when we inhale. Never think of "taking a breath in" because it will tense up and contract your upper muscular girth. Rather approach this action by *allowing* the air to come into your body.

### Suggested Experiments

The following list of different experiments is designed to stimulate, feel, and develop the diaphragm.

- Tonic, hypotonic, hypertonic reference.
- 20% natural **organic breathing** and 40% or condition breathing.
- Astronaut Experiment.
- Phase I–VIII.
- Astronaut Against the Wall.
- Foo Dog.

### Diaphragm Stretch Experiment

One of the simplest and most natural ways to do this is to hang from a sturdy tree branch or pull up bar, making sure your shoulders do not go up by your ears covering your cervical belt. Allow your shoulders to remain down. Still hanging from the branch or bar, exhale a long, deep, slow breath with fully dropped Shower Mouth. Inhale on six counts (one–two–three nose/abdomen and four–five–six Shower Mouth/Gills). Exhale naturally or on nine counts using Tempered Breath.

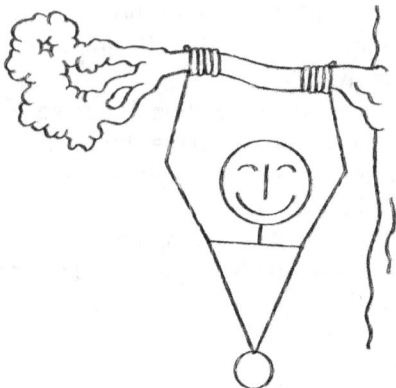

*Figure 4.29* Imagine stretching your diaphragm by hanging off a tree branch.

You can also do a similar stretch by lying in supine position on the floor doing the same exhalation but having your arms raised over your head resting on the floor. Make sure that all your vertebrae, lumbar and sacrum included, are in contact with the floor. You may need to bend your elbows slightly if straightening your arms forces an arch in your lumbar. Your feet are flexed off the floor, with your thighs close to your chest and your knees pointing towards your chin.

### The Abdomen

The abdomen is located between the thorax and the pelvis. It contains all the digestive organs of the body. These organs are connected by a supple membrane called the mesentery. The diaphragm separates the abdomen from the thorax.

Having a well-toned abdominal core is essential for general health, as well as for the spine. However, the constant assault and bombardment of "the six pack" or "washboard abs" culture does not consider the importance of a relaxed lower abdomen. Abdominal or conditioned breathing maximizes the amount of oxygen in our blood, and it is imperative for supporting a healthy voice.

Since the chest cavity is relatively "rigid" with bones, when the diaphragm contracts it pushes down the viscera into the abdominal cavity.

Because we have many sensory receptors in the abdomen, we feel and see the domino effect of its muscular activity in our low bellies, but that is not the diaphragm. There is a common misconception that the diaphragm is situated in the abdomen. That concept is erroneous. In fact, what we see is the result of the compression that the diaphragm causes in the abdomen when it contracts during our inhale.

The abdominal muscles and the diaphragm are antagonistic; thus, when one muscle contracts, the other muscle relaxes. The abdominal muscles assist us with the exhale more than with the inhale. Soliciting and engaging the abdominal muscles with the inhale is not a good idea because it creates unnecessary pressure and tension in our larynx.

## The Mesentery

The mesentery is a fan-shaped membrane (peritoneum) in the abdomen that attaches the intestine to the abdominal wall to hold it in place. It encloses in its fold the abdominal viscera; within it, there are arteries, veins, nerves, and lymph nodes that supply the intestine. In 2016, the mesentery was reclassified in the medical world as a single organ. It plays an important role in the intestinal, vascular, endocrine, cardiovascular, and immunological systems. I, in all my innocence, see a very strong potential connection between this organ and the notion of **Dantien**.

## The Dantien (Tan Tien)

**Dantien** in Chinese, or *Hara* in Japanese, is not always an easy concept to grasp for the Western mind. The *Dantien* is associated with a more subtle way of understanding the body (physical, emotional, mental, spiritual) and the body's energy as practiced in many cultures from the East: Buddhist and Taoist practices, Tai Chi Chu'an, tea ceremonies, calligraphy, martial arts, kyudo, aikido, meditation breathing techniques, qigong, acupuncture, reiki, and Chinese traditional medicine, amongst many others.

Though not anatomically identifiable, the *Dantien* is that region in the human body situated 1.5–2.5 inches below and 1.5 inches behind the navel, around the level of our sacro-lumbar hinge (L-5/S-1). About the size of a ping-pong or tennis ball, it can act as the major gate regulator and distributor of energy in the body.[9]

It is often referred to in the practices I mentioned above as: the center, center of gravity, neuralgic center, center of vital energy, reflex brain, second brain, source of power, storage of energy, a leaning point, sea of energy, anchor, alchemical cauldron, cinnabar center, field of elixir, field of healing, reservoir of "chi" energy, or *hara*.

All martial arts or somatic energy base practices require a connection to this center.

The *Dantien* can only be opened or stimulated by a deep, persistent, and well-developed sense of awareness, as well as consistent and rigorous control of the physical body.[10]

Opening the *Dantien* implies a "sinking" or letting go of muscular strength; only then can it bring forth the necessary physical balance for stability on the ground. Deep abdominal breathing and concentration favors the activation and accumulation of energy. Activation and opening of one's *Dantien* can result in the deepening of one's ability for self-development as well as improvement of one's health.

When you give your attention to the *Dantien*, your thoughts slow down and allow you to attain a stronger sense of serenity, stability, and energized centering.

### *Opening Dantien Experiment*

1) In demi-plié, on second position, alternate "micro shakes" of the pelvis in all directions for four beats, with four counts of rest, providing your body with muscular tonicity.
2) Your spine should be lengthened, your arms slightly bent in front of your iliac crest level describing alternative centrifugal circles as if you were spreading flour on a table the size of a large pizza tray. You will use both clockwise and counterclockwise motion, depending on the hand, to create centrifugal (outward) circles.
3) On a second variation, shift the diameter of the circles by making them smaller: the size of a pancake.

4) On a third variation, you will make even smaller circles the size of a small DVD. Avoid **"body chatter"** in the rest of the body as you do this. You achieve this by mindfully putting weight on the outsides of your feet.
5) Now repeat the same experiment with centripetal motion of the arms, instead of centrifugal, and the varying circle sizes.

## The Pelvis

The pelvic cavity is formed by the sacrum, coccyx, and hipbones. Its primary function is to support the pelvic viscera as well as to transmit strength to the bones along the body's long axis and to the lower limbs.

The pelvic floor, or pelvic diaphragm, is composed of muscles as well as connective tissues covering the area underneath the pelvis. It separates the pelvic cavity, above, from the **perineal** region, below. This area also supports the muscles underneath the abdominal and pelvic viscera.

From a muscular point of view, imagine this area as an inverted dome, a wok, or a cauldron attached to the pelvis, holding the abdominal viscera. The pelvic floor not only has to hold the weight of the viscera, but it also must manage pressure generated in the lower part of the abdomen during breathing, coughing, urination, defecation, birth, sexual intercourse, and of course, while using one's voice.

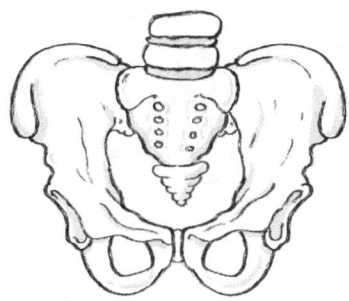

*Figure 4.30* The pelvis.

The lungs create pressure on the vocal folds and the participation of the abdominal muscles takes place not only upwards but also downwards, thus affecting the perineum.

This pressure encounters a break in the flow of the glottis, which is almost entirely closed during phonation. This pressure is felt and sent downwards to the pelvic floor. The pelvic floor therefore not only supports the pressures addressed to it, but also actively participates in the muscles that create the necessary upward pressure.

### Union Jack Experiment

For Conditioned Breathing training, practice sitting in the yoga's "tailor position" using Buddha Belly/Inner Tube. It is important that you encourage the feeling and the perception of the expansion of your perineal region against the floor. This naturally occurs when the diaphragm pushes down the abdominal mass, a feeling like when we cough, the beginning of defecation, or the clearing of the throat. I often encourage students to imagine the pelvic floor expanding outwards in the same way as the bands that form the Union Jack flag, or like a spot of olive oil being absorbed by a paper napkin.

*Figure 4.31* Imagine your pelvic floor expanding like the bands of Great Britain's Union Jack.

### Psoas Muscle

The psoas muscle is critical for our alignment. In Chinese tradition, the psoas muscle, together with the Dantien, are both considered anchors of the soul. A tight psoas makes our breathing shallow, causes back pain, digestive problems, and neck pain. It is a long muscle located on the side of the lumbar area of the spine and the rim of the pelvis. It originates between the first and fourth lumbar vertebrae and the twelfth thoracic vertebrae. It joins together several deep pelvic muscles that impact our muscular and skeletal balance.

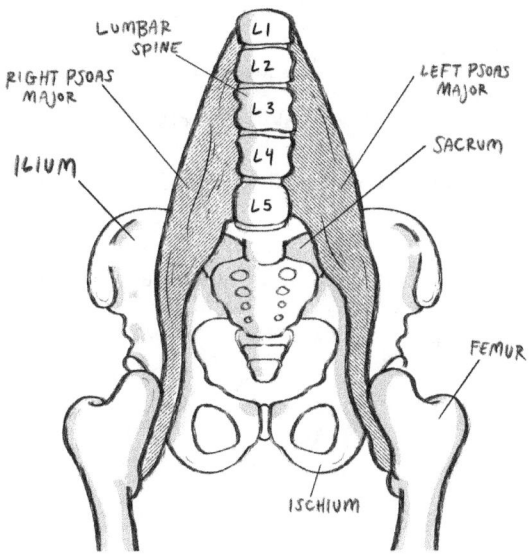

*Figure 4.32* Anatomy of the psoas muscle.

The psoas muscle also affects the fluidity and flexibility of the pelvis as a primal center of energy. It plays a major role in stabilizing the lumbar spine and area. The psoas is the prime flexor of the hip joint connecting the vertebral column to the legs. It attaches to the top of the femur. This very important muscle helps keep us straight and determines the gait of our walk. The psoas connects with the diaphragm and therefore is particularly involved in conditioned breathing.

If it contracts, it shortens the distance between the pubis and the navel, bringing the lumbar spine forward.

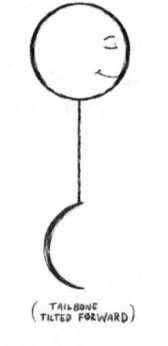

**CONCAVE PELVIS**

*Figure 4.33* A concave/forward-tilting pelvis.

If it hyperextends, it makes the pelvis retract, creating excessive spinal curve (lordosis).

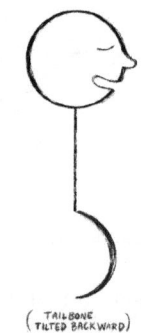

**CONVEX PELVIS**

*Figure 4.34* A convex/backward-tilting pelvis.

### Preparation for the Experiments

Lie down on your back. Use tempered breath. When you inhale (three counts through abdomen/nose and three through Shower

Mouth/Gills), allow all your vertebrae to drop and be in contact with the floor. As you exhale, allow your lumbar-sacrum area to create a bridge as if water could flow easily from right to left underneath it without any obstacle. Each cycle will have at least nine comfortable counts of tempered exhale. This encourages your gills and your Inner Tube/Buddha Belly to work in synergy.

### *Astronaut Against the Wall Experiment*

1) Lie down on your back. Feet with legs, legs with knees, knees with thighs, thighs with hips, each set at a 90° angle to one another. Your feet leaning but not pushing against the wall (as if you were sitting in a perfect chair and the wall is the floor underneath you). It is key that you investigate the very important difference between pushing against the wall (which you absolutely do not want to do) and leaning (known in singing as 'appoggio') or engaging your weight against the wall, which is what you do want to do.
2) Allow your breath to cascade into you with ease (three counts for low abdomen/nose and three for Shower Mouth/Gills); ideally, all your vertebrae will end up dropping into contact with the floor.
3) As soon as you start inhaling, your heels should lean/engage slightly further into the wall. Again, this is not a push but a feeling in your heels of gaining extra surface due to the slight leaning you give into the wall. This assists and engages the participation of your pelvic floor, your abdomen, and the diaphragm simultaneously.
4) During the inhaling, your arms start by your sides, and they are going to slide gently on the floor, moving away from your hips, until you reach a 45° angle, or inverted 10:10 position by the end of the six inhaling counts.
5) Use News prior to and throughout the duration of the experiment. All the vertebrae against the floor. Your pelvis is slightly **concave**.

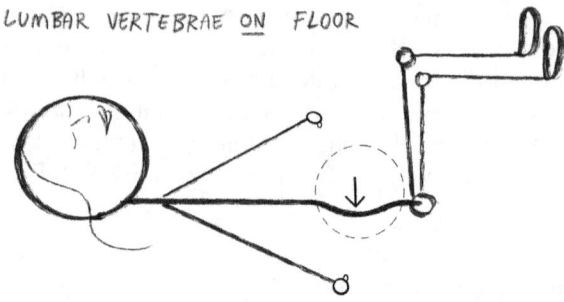

*Figure 4.35* Lumbar vertebrae slightly concave on inhaling.

6) For the exhale, release your tempered breath with the sound of "s." Allow your pelvis to tilt slowly forward as your lumbar area lifts off the floor creating a small bridge under which an imaginary brook could run through. Your arms move simultaneously from the inverted 10:10 position you started on, to end up by your sides. Use News as you breathe out. The pelvis during the exhaling becomes slightly **convex**.

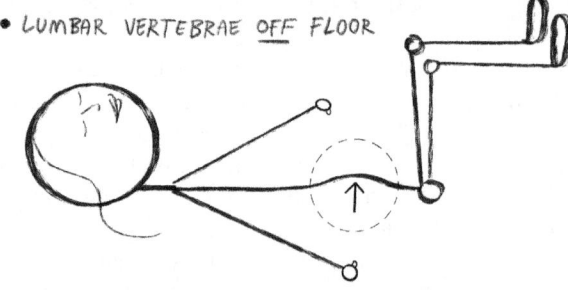

*Figure 4.36* Lumbar vertebrae slightly convex on exhaling.

7) Repeat the experiment several times not only with tempered breath on "s" but also on "NG" and "NGA" using Backyard/Tongue #3 at 40%.

## Standing-Up Astronaut Experiment

1) Coordinate abdominal and intercostal Conditioned Breathing (six counts for inhaling and nine at least for exhaling).
2) Stand with your back one to two feet away from the wall. Soften your knees to free your pelvis and allow your body to rest against the wall, giving your weight into it somewhat. You should be about one inch shorter than your regular height. It is imperative that you maintain this height throughout the experiment.
3) Your scapulae and glutes are touching the wall because you are leaning against the wall. Comb your hair upwards to free and lengthen your neck. Very important: your nape does not have to touch the wall (due to the unavoidable curvature of your neck). Avoid creating "guillotine/pelican" neck. You can use if you like a small bean bag, a folded T-shirt, or handkerchief to serve as a mini pillow for you to rest your head against the wall.
4) Inhale, allowing the air to cascade into you with the image of Inner Tube/Buddha Belly (three counts for the nose/abdomen, three for your Shower Mouth/Gills). All dorsal and lumbar vertebrae should be in contact with the wall during inhaling, but not the cervical. Your pelvis is also against the wall. As you articulate your spine in this experiment, the height you acquired when sitting against the wall should never change.
5) Exhale (nine counts at least on tempered "s" breath) and allow the pelvis to rock/tilt back leaving the contact you had with the wall. Think of your gills/floating ribs expanding on the axis of 9:15 on a clock, without collapsing.
6) Do this slowly and gently, without contracting the pelvis or changing the height of your body. Your pelvis has created during the exhalation a concave bridge off the wall at the level of your sacrum/lumbar area.

## Imagery

- Opening and closing big bellows, an accordion, or a shoji screen being unfolded/opened simultaneously in opposite directions.

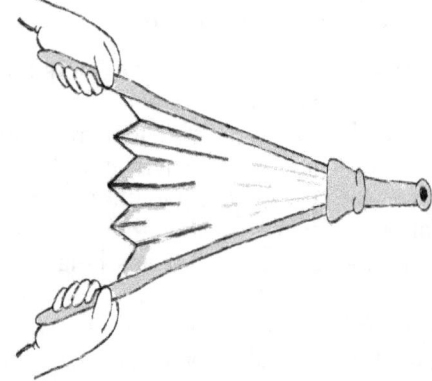

*Figure 4.37* Imagine you are opening and closing bellows to expand and release your breathing.

### Slow-Motion Astronaut Spacewalk Experiment

1) Slow-motion walk, reminiscent of **suriashi Noh walk**. Always maintain your height one inch lower than your natural height by bending your knees. Maintain your pelvis and head during your walk on the same plane levels. Front leg flexed and the back leg lengthened.

*Figure 4.38* Maintain an even, slow-motion walk, like an astronaut's spacewalk.

2) All your weight is on the front leg while you begin to inhale (six counts), sliding simultaneously the other foot, in full contact with the floor (suriashi Noh walk). Continue inhaling and bringing the back foot forward to join the other foot by lifting it up until its heel reaches the level of the opposite knee.
3) Exhale (six to nine counts) bringing the back foot forward and placing it down one foot ahead of the planted foot. Transfer the weight to that newly forward foot and repeat the action, alternating feet each step.
4) Your arms go out to inverted 10:10 during your inhale and they revert to being by your sides during the exhale.

### Pelvis and Psoas Tonification Experiment

1) Lying on your back on the floor, flex your legs 90° up in the air as for the astronaut position without touching the wall at all this time.
2) Engage your muscles only in a tonic manner, never hyper-contracting them. This means just before the point when you feel a light tremor/trembling in your abdominal low muscles, like the feeling of a sewing machine's needle pounding the fabric with stitches.

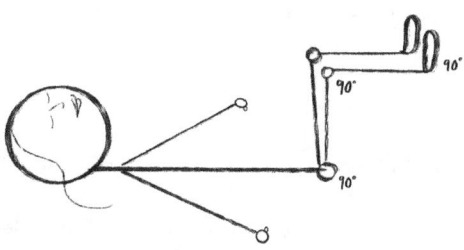

*Figure 4.39* Engagement of your core with your lumbar vertebrae lying on the floor.

3) Grab your thighs from behind the knees. Your legs want to go back to the floor but do not allow them to do so.

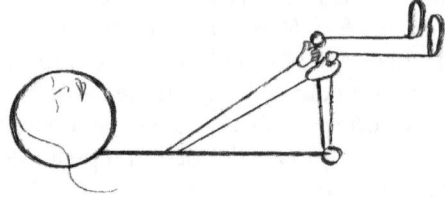

· HANDS BEHIND THE KNEES

*Figure 4.40* Hands assisting the back of your knees.

4) Your palms are placed on the lower thighs, close to your kneecaps. Resist the pressure that the thighs are applying against your hands. Do not allow them to come towards your face. Breathe naturally.

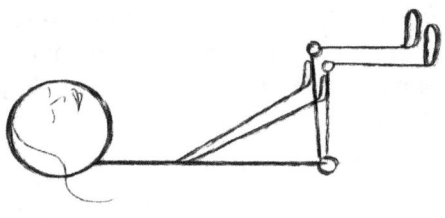

· HANDS ON THIGHS

*Figure 4.41* Hands resisting against the push of your thighs.

5) Place your hands now outside your knees. Your legs will want to fan out to the sides but do not let them. Breathe naturally.

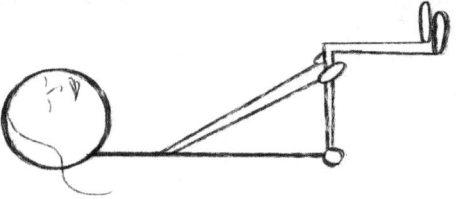

· HANDS ON THE SIDE OF THE KNEES.

*Figure 4.42* Hands resisting the falling out of the knees.

# Sound Grounding 75

6) Place both your fists side by side between your knees. Your legs want to shorten that distance in between them but do not allow it. Breathe naturally.

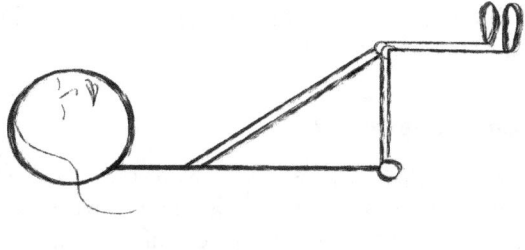

*Figure 4.43* Fists inside the knees resisting them approaching each other.

## Pelvis and Psoas Release Experiment

1) Stand up sideways on top of a bench or a staircase step. Soften the knees. Shake gently but firmly, as if dead weight, the leg over the edge of the bench or the step.
2) After a minute or so, swing the leg back and forth like a nice, relaxed clock pendulum. Avoid applying force. Do this several times.
3) Before you change sides give yourself the chance to walk some steps on the floor so that you can perceive the difference in the leg length you just swung. You will feel that the leg you just swung feels slightly longer.

## Perineal Call Experiment

1) Sit in "tailor position." Your spine is aligned and lengthened with ease. Your weight is distributed evenly on your sitz bones. No force is being applied.
2) Inhale and feel your Inner Tube/ Buddha Belly (six counts), allowing your perineal area to spread its contact with the floor as you exhale with Conditioned Breath (nine counts).

## Imagery

- When inhaling: as if a large balloon on the floor is being filled with water.
- When exhaling: as if an oil spot is spreading slowly and progressively on a paper napkin.

## Dantien Call Experiment

1) In plié second position, as if you were riding a horse, shake internally (in other words not showing to anyone that you are making your body shake) for four counts your pelvis and buttocks in all directions without clenching them or changing your height.
2) Then suspend the action for another four counts while you call upon your Dantien, and mindfully bring your attention to the weight on the outside of the feet. This re-enlivens your Dantien. Make sure that your spine is fully lengthened.

## Grounding: Pelvis and Feet Calls Experiment

Your pelvis and feet connect and support your voice when you align the spine. This experiment is inspired by Spanish flamenco "taconeo/zapateao" with the fundamental difference that we will be using the ensemble of the foot to stomp on the floor using specific voice calls, not just the heels. This helps to center, ground, and invigorate our sound production.

Over the years I have created a simple series of rhythmic stomping patterns in a circle, accentuating different beats on an 8- and 12-count rhythmic structure using vocalizations alternating on the stomping's "NGA" and **Image Words**. Your height is to be one inch shorter (soften your knees) than your actual height so that your spine absorbs the stomping shocks without hurting your body. This position is also reminiscent of some martial arts practices.

In rehearsal, much inspired by Peter Brook, I often add the use of dowels to accompany a variety of rhythmic sequences and dowel throwing variations to enliven one's individual voice projection as well as to develop and create a collective sense of awareness and ensemble energy.

## Notes

1. Moshé Feldenkrais is a Ukrainian–Israeli engineer and physicist. He is known as the founder of the Feldenkrais Method, a system of physical exercise that works to improve human functioning by increasing self-awareness through movement.
2. For more extensive material relative to the gaze, I strongly recommend reading the chapter on "Face and Eyes" of "The Secret Art of the Performer" by Eugenio Barba & Nicola Savarese.
3. A thin, elastic sheath of connective fibrous tissue enveloping most structures in the body, including muscles.
4. The epiglottis is like a lid that protects the trachea or windpipe from having food and fluids enter it.
5. I prefer to use "pronunciation" versus "articulation" because in my experience I observed that whenever I say in Spanish, French, or English: "let me hear you pronounce the word(s) . . ." vs. "let me hear you articulate the word(s) . . ." the performer approaches the delivery differently. When I use "pronounce," the performer's intent appears to privilege how to chain together the syllables in the word or the phrase, connecting them much like the natural flow of a river. When I use "articulate," people seem to target it more in a didactic manner, "chopping up" or "isolating" the sounds more like levees in a river. Articulation encourages a certain mechanical self-consciousness, while pronunciation softens that attitude.
6. Its name comes from the Greek "thyreoeides" which means shield.
7. The glottis or the glottal passage is the part of the larynx consisting of the vocal folds and the opening between them.
8. Apnea is a temporary suspension or interruption of our breathing. Naturally there are two types of apnea, one at the end of inhalation and the other at the end of exhalation.
9. The Taoist concept of *Dantiens* as an energy center is not so different from the concept of chakras in yoga. They both consider this place as a seminal location in the body where *prana* (life-force, or breath) is saved and collected. The term *Dantien* is also equivalent to the Japanese word *hara*, which means "belly." In Chinese, Korean, and Japanese traditions, the *Dantien* is considered the physical center of gravity of the human body and the source of one's chi or internal energy.
10. Opening one's *Dantien* is a long process that takes years of regular training. It is interesting to point out the major differences between the East and the West cultures in representing the divine. The former relies on the presence of a lengthened back and a sticking out belly, while the latter fosters a low, flat abdomen pulled in and up like a washboard.

# Chapter 5

# The Industry of Breath and Alignment

## On Breath

### *"Don't 'Take' a Breath In!"*

Regardless of the type of breathing we do, it is important to consider a couple of points.

Remember that to inhale can also be referred to as to "inspire;" in this way to "breathe in" is a way to attract, allure, or draw air into our bodies. Inspiring is a way to allow the air to return to us. Breathing in air can also be thought of as the quality or state of being renewed; the influence that can move the brain, the intellect, the mind; the process of being stimulated or the act of doing something new or creative.

Inspiration is also about inventiveness, ingenuity, beginning, insight, imagination, originality, creativity, innovation, vision, risk, and initiative.

For all these reasons, I never advise my students to think of it as simply "take" a breath in. The return of air to the lungs should be related to what has just been "spent". It is that simple. It is not about how much air can be taken into the body, but rather about how much air must be returned to the body in response to what has been spoken, sung, or breathed.

It is counter-productive and counter-intuitive to have the attitude of "I am going to take in as much air as I can for my next tirade." It tenses one up. It short-circuits our ability to have a healthy relationship with our own breath and the imagination.

Letting the air come into our bodies should be a passive reflex action, not an active driven one. Allow the air to "cascade" into you rather than "taking" it in. When we inhale, all that should happen is that: an inhale occurring simply, organically, and inevitably. What we need to learn is our exhale and how to train it.

Focusing on what we "give out" (breathing out) will make us automatically bring more air into our lungs after. is not so different from the notion that "the more you give, the more you will receive."

Make sure that when you inspire, you inhale, remaining porous and permeable. As you do so, pay attention to the sensations of the air reaching you inside or allow pleasant news.

### Organic Versus Conditioned Breathing

Whether you are breathing organically, as in daily life, or conditioned, for the stage, the diaphragm participates in your breathing all the time. The fundamental difference lies in whether you call for the diaphragm's support on your exhale or not. I refer to this action as *tempering your breath with your diaphragm*, similar to tempering a guitar with the tuning pegs.

The final control of your breath relies on your mind and your feelings, but we are going to see fundamentally two different breathing patterns that are very relevant to the performer. One happens naturally in daily life, while the other is designed for the stage.

The following experiments are going to show you, experientially, when you are supporting the sound with the activation of your diaphragm and when you are not.

### Organic Breathing

This breathing is based on the observation of the breath of a naturally healthy infant being properly looked after, well fed, nurtured, played with, and pampered. As adults, we develop a breathing pattern that is influenced by our early life experiences and may not always be natural or healthy. The good news is that we can restore it back to its natural healthy state of being.

Think of a baby lying down on its back. As the baby breathes in, the pelvis naturally tilts slightly forwards anteversion, creating a subtle arch, like a bridge on the lumbar area. As the baby breathes out, the reverse will happen. The lumbar area of the pelvis tilts slightly back, like a wok or a cauldron. We call this retroversion.

### Organic Breathing Experiment

The 20% breath – I use the term "organic" as in: innate, instinctive, ordinary.

*Figure 5.1* A cascading waterfall at 20% for organic breathing.

This is the breathing we do automatically in daily life. The diaphragm works on its own, without us interfering with it. I qualify it as a 20% breath to convey the image and feeling that we do not employ work/effort for it to happen. It simply happens. In this breathing the diaphragm contracts and relaxes involuntarily, like a long seaweed undulating in calm waters, like a waterfall or cascades.

1) Stand in your Relative Position.
2) Have a straw. Place it between your lips as when you draw water from a glass.
3) Place your hands on your lower abdomen, between your navel and pubis.
4) Inhale and let the air come in through the nose freely, without effort. Avoid holding your breath.
5) On your exhale, let the air simply go out by itself through the straw.

### Notice

- How on the inhaling your belly expanded and how naturally it reacted on the exhaling, slightly flattening.
- In other words, if your waistline is 30 inches by the end of the inhale, as you exhale naturally and progressively it will go from 30 to 29.5–29–28.5–28.
- There is a sense in your body as if this action was happening above the straw, behind the nose so to speak.

### Imagery

- A waterfall, cascades.
- Smoke from a chimney.
- Water pouring out from a jug.

### Cow and the Halloween Cat Experiment

1) Inhale:

On all fours, have the image of a cow breathing in, grazing in the pasture. Direct your gaze to the floor 5–6 feet in front of you. There is synergy and synchronicity in between the breath and the subtle natural movement of the arching of the spine. The movement should always initiate in the tailbone as you breathe in, and it follows vertebrae by vertebrae through the spine until reaching the occiput (summit of your cranium). You are creating a ripple in a slow, gentle motion. In this action, the pelvis is tilted forward on anteversion. Your chin and tailbone are the furthest away. So "the cow breathes in."

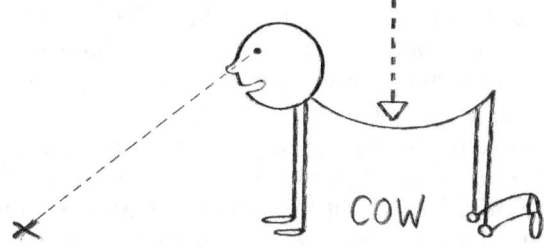

*Figure 5.2* Cow inhaling position with proper gaze.

## 2) Exhale:

On the outbreath we reverse the previous pattern. We still initiate the movement in the tailbone, but this time it is going to have the opposite swiping motion. As if it was to shorten the distance between chin and tailbone. In this action the pelvis is caving in retroversion. The chin and tailbone are the closest. The spine is reminiscent of a hissing Halloween cat silhouette. So "the 'Halloween cat' breathes out."

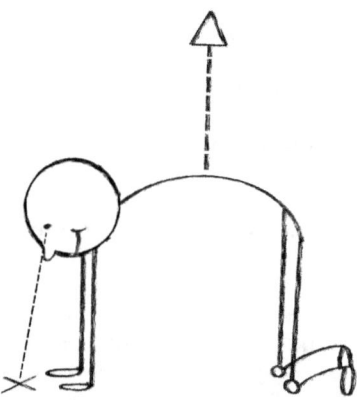

*Figure 5.3* Cat exhaling position with proper gaze.

### Conditioned Breathing

This is the ideal breathing we want to practice, supporting and strengthening our work on stage without hurting ourselves.

When practicing Conditioned Breathing, all your vertebrae are going to be in contact with that floor. There is going to be a subtle retroversion of the pelvis in your inhale and a retroversion on the exhale. In this type of breathing, we are going to encourage your "Gills" or the Intercostal muscles to participate considerably. By doing this, you are giving the diaphragm more space to contract downwards but also laterally. The result is that you are maximizing the torso's potential expansion up, down, and sideways; therefore, increasing the lungs capacity or air-volume.

## Conditioned Breathing Experiment

The 40% breath – I use the term "conditioned" because it is the opposite of what is natural, untrained, and comfortable. Conditioned Breathing as in *trained, adapted, adjusted,* or *acclimated.*

*Figure 5.4* A flame blowing out at 40% for Conditioned Breathing.

In this form of breathing, we are going to call consciously on our diaphragm during the exhale. I double the percentage to 40% to give you the sense that there is labor involved in it. Here we are voluntarily soliciting the active participation of the diaphragm for our exhale. We want to do this to overcome the natural obstacles that occur in our voice and body when we come into the artificial space of the stage.

1) Place the straw in your mouth and your hands on the lower abdomen.
2) This time the image you are going to have when you exhale is of blowing out a candle that is 5–7 feet straight ahead of you.
3) As you exhale make sure that you "see" the flickering of the flame because of the strength of your breath).

### Notice:

- How your lower abdomen muscles (transverse, obliques, and the abdominal muscle) have tonified due to you actively blowing the candle out.

- This tonification is exactly what you want to feel when you need to support your breath on stage.
- In other words, as we did before, if your waistline is 30 inches by the end of the inhale, on this exhale you will actively want to support the diaphragm to maintain the size of 30 inches for a number of seconds before the abdomen flattens naturally as you are running out of breath.
- There is a sense in your body of feeling this work below the straw, in your upper, middle, and lower abdomen.

### Astronaut Experiment

I chose this name for the experiment because of the immense amount of training that astronauts must subject themselves to in order to attain the unimaginable feat of setting foot on the moon. To embody and integrate this type of breathing is not so dissimilar to me as it requires perseverance and resilience.

Lie down on your back with your feet against the wall. Your legs, knees, thighs, and hips should all be at a 90° angle. It is key that you investigate the important difference in your feet between pushing against the wall, which you absolutely do not want to do, and leaning or engaging ('appoggio'[1]) against the wall, which is what you want to do.

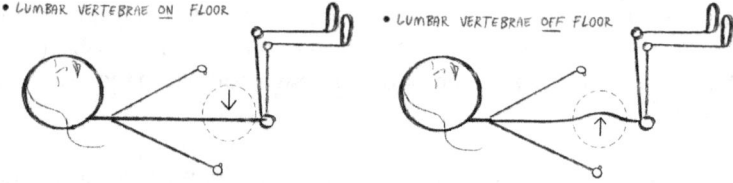

Figure 5.5.a and 5.5.b Lumbar vertebrae in the Astronaut Experiment.

Inhale:

1) All your vertebrae are in contact with the floor as you allow the air to cascade into your body.
2) Use six counts for the inhaling (Counts 1, 2, 3 are for Inner Tube/Buddha Belly (low abdominal area) through your nose

and the last three (Counts 4, 5, 6) for your Gills (Intercostal area) through Shower Mouth. Your pelvis is stabilized.
3) Your arms, resting on the floor by your sides, are going to move away from your hips towards the inverted 10:10 position, simultaneously and synchronically as your breath cascades into your body with ease.
4) You are breathing in without contracting your muscles. Buddha Belly/Inner Tube manifests front and sides in your lower abdomen. Let the breath reach effortlessly to your inner body. Avoid taking a breath by forcing it into your body. Use Image/News prior to and during your inhaling. The lumbar area of your pelvis on the floor is slightly concave.

Exhale:

1) Exhale on nine counts at least. As soon as you start exhaling, the heels of your feet should lean/engage slightly into the wall. Again, this is not a push but a feeling of your heels having more surface contact with the wall.
2) This helps you to engage at once your diaphragm, your abdomen, and your pelvic floor. At that same moment you should start releasing your tempered breath with the sound of "s" at 40%.
3) Allow your lumbar area to get off the floor, as if creating a subtle bridge under which a river could run through. Your arms move simultaneously with your breath going inwards and ending by your side. The lumbar area of your pelvis, without using force simply releasing, is slightly convex.
4) Repeat the experiment several times not only with tempered breath on "s" at 40% but also on "NG" and "NGA" with Tongue #3.

## Inner Tube, Buddha Belly, Low Abdominal Breathing

An **inner tube** is the device we use to help people to float, move and play in the water before they are capable of swimming on their own.

I use this image because if we, as performers, do not allow our abdomen to expand naturally and sustain that enlargement, we will fail in the face of obstacles that are presented to us on stage.

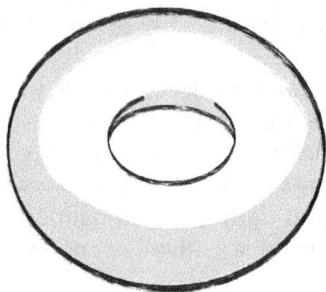

*Figure 5.6* Donut/Inner Tube representing ideal abdominal breathing.

Therefore, I encourage my students to visualize this low abdominal breathing with the following images: Inner Tube, Buddha Belly, a large donut, or Monsieur and Madame Michelin.

Having a well-toned abdominal core is very effective for both your health and your spine. However, the constant assault and bombardment of the hypertonic "six-pack chocolate bar or washboard iron belly" in Western culture does not consider how important is to have a well-relaxed, available low abdomen. The expansion of your relaxed low abdomen will maximize the amount of oxygen intake coming from your blood stream.

As we inhale, the abdominal muscles expand in opposition as the diaphragm contracts. They assist us more in the exhale than in the inhale. To solicit and engage them when we inhale is not a good idea because of the potential of creating unnecessary force and tension.

The common misunderstanding in popular culture is to think that the diaphragm is situated in the abdomen. Anatomically, the diaphragm separates the thorax from the abdomen. Since the chest cavity is relatively "rigid" with bones and we have a lot of sensory receptors in the abdomen, when the diaphragm contracts, the abdominal viscera are compressed down and all around the abdominal cavity. The natural outcome of this is the expansion of the abdomen. What we see and feel is the domino effect caused by the diaphragm in the abdomen, not the diaphragm itself. The proper use of the diaphragm on stage unites the voice and the body, therefore integrating the mind of the performer.

### Areas of the Conditioned Breathing

The following experiment is designed to differentiate the successive steps regarding the expansion of our abdominothoracic areas as we allow the air to come into our bodies. In looking at the diagram below, it is essential to understand how certain body cavities play a role in our Conditioned Breathing. It is crucial to imagine the Cranial Cavity, and above the cranium, as one of the potential locations for producing Air sounds. The other four cavities are present in both Organic and Conditioned Breathing. However, it is of the utmost importance for Conditioned Breathing to consider the low pelvic cavity, the middle abdominal cavity, and the upper girth/thoracic cavity. These four cavities participate exceptionally in abdominal/Intercostal Conditioned Breathing.

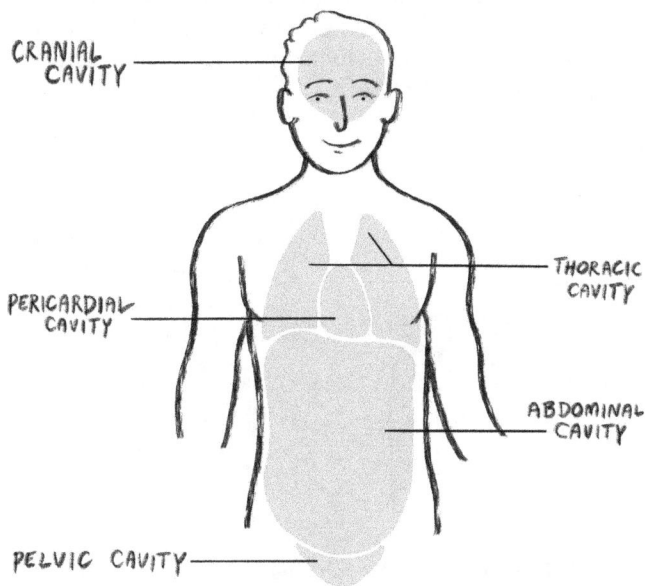

Figure 5.7 Five cavities of the body.

### Gills with Conditioned Breathing Experiment

As the Sanskrit proverb says, *"For breath is life, and if you breathe well, you will live long on earth."*

1) Lay on the floor facing up or legs crossed in tailor sitting position.
2) Inhale on six counts:

   The first three counts are through the nose/abdomen connection and last three counts through Shower Mouth/Gills connection.

   Counts 1, 2, and 3: Low Abdominal/Inner Tube/Buddha Belly.
   Counts 4, 5, and 6: Upper Thoracic/Intercostal/Upper Girth.

3) Exhale on nine counts:

   Release your breath with ease with tempered breath on "s" at 40%. Allow your Gills to fan out if you comfortably can before they close into your sides with the motion like that of slow motion blowing out bellows.

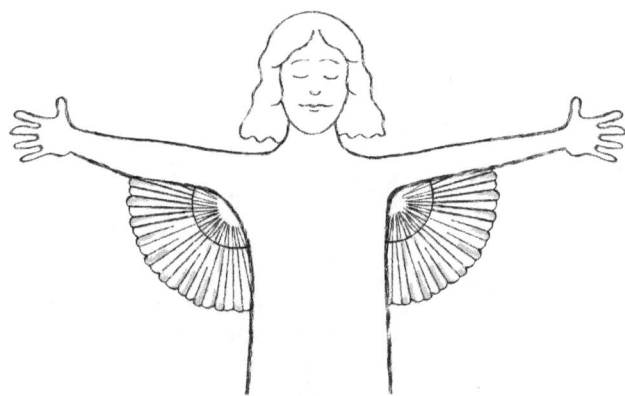

*Figure 5.8* Gills fanning out for inhaling.

### Your Shakespeare Works "On You" Experiment

*A healthy mind has an easy breath.*

This is a very traditional way to encourage abdominal breathing from your lower abdomen.

Put your Shakespeare book (it really can be any book with some weight) between your navel and your pubis. Allow it to rise gently as you inhale. Allow the book to stay there as you exhale for as long as your **amber light** permits. Your amber light is the moment your brain sends the message, "It is time to let new air into your body, take a new breath."

### Kinesthetic Diaphragm Experiment: Friction-ing Hands

This experiment is designed fundamentally to provide you with proprioception of the diaphragm.

1) Stand in Relative Position. Inhale and gently rub the palms of your hands together in a circular motion creating friction for 30 seconds.
2) Stop, rest, and release a vocalized sigh.
3) Now stand in a Broadway 7 position (see Figure 6.9) and vigorously rub your palms together creating friction. As your arms lengthen, move in all possible directions around you. Do this for 45 seconds as far away from you as you can while moving away from your original spot.
4) Stop the action, rest, and release deliberately, with volume (medium loud) on a vocalized sigh.

### Notice:

- What differences did you feel between the two different ways of sighing?
- Could you perceive the diaphragm supporting your sound when you did this the second time around?

### Kinesthetic Diaphragm Experiment: The Pelvis Rudder

Lay facing up with all vertebrae in contact with the floor. Pelvis stabilized. Grab both feet with your hands. Imagine you have the rudder of a boat in your hands.

1) Inhale:

On six counts (one–two–three for abdomen/nose and four–five–six for Shower Mouth/Gills). Slightly bring your feet closer to your chin. You are pulling the rudder off the water. Allow your tailbone to get off the floor.

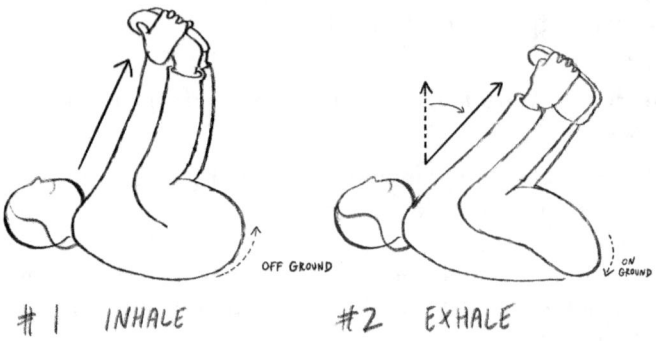

Figure 5.9 The two positions for the Pelvis Rudder.

2) Exhale:

On nine counts and do the reverse, by now bringing the rudder into the water. Allow the tailbone to be flat on the floor. You may need to adjust your feet as you release them.

Feel the connection between the tilting of the pelvis and the Conditioned Breathing patterns you use.

### Kinesthetic Diaphragm Experiment: The Wok and Frog

This experiment encourages proprioception of the abdominal area, the pelvic floor, and the Gills/Intercostal areas:

1) Lay facing up arms on an inverted 10:10. Heels together in first ballet position but with your legs flexed towards your pelvis (see drawing) like a frog. Feel the gentle rocking motion of the wok (your pelvis).
2) Observe the two inhaling stages over a six-count pattern.

The Industry of Breath and Alignment   91

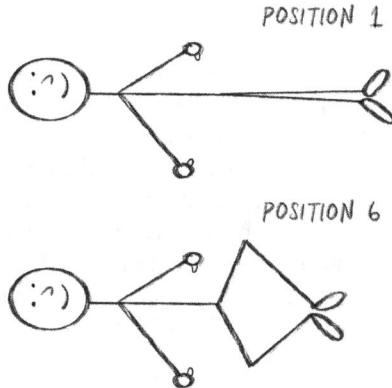

*Figure 5.10* Positions for the Wok and Frog.

- First set of three counts through the nose focusing on the pelvis and abdomen.
- The final three counts through Shower Mouth privileging the Gills/Intercostals.

3) Exhale over nine counts with tempered breath on "s" at 40% and News. You do not need to use arms in this experiment. Simply focus on the proprioception for the pelvis, the spine, and the Intercostal/Gills expansion.

Variation #1:

1) Your body stands up on second plié position as if you were riding on horseback. Use fiction, keep your spine aligned, have your pelvic floor supporting your breath, and have your arms relaxed by your sides.
2) Inhale on six counts (one–two–three counts through your nose/low abdomen, four–five–six counts through your Shower Mouth/Gills).

   Make sure your inhaling is gentle, so you feel the outward opening of the mid-section of your Gill/Intercostal area, as well as between your shoulder blades.
3) Exhale on nine counts with tempered breath on "s" at 40% and News. You can repeat the experiment both on "NG" and "NGA."

Variation #2:

1) Do the same as in the previous experiment; however, to increase abdominal–thoracic–breathing proprioception, allow the arms to lengthen and move up by your side as you inhale. Your arms should end up with your wrists below your shoulders on the inverted 10:10 by the end of Count 6.
2) Exhale on nine counts on 40% with tempered breath on "s" and News. You can repeat the experiment both on "NG" and "NGA" as your arms simultaneously accompany your breathing to end up in your starting position.

Variation #3:

1) Everyone's body is different. This variation will be for those who feel this work on the abdomen and intercostals better by allowing their arms to end up on the sixth count above their head. Use the image of the handles of a clock striking 12:00.
   Be very mindful as your arms end up above your head that your shoulders and scapulae connection remain firmly down.
2) Exhale on nine counts on 40% with tempered breath on "s" and News. You can repeat the experiment both on "NG" and "NGA" as your arms simultaneously accompany your breathing to end up in your starting position.

Please verify, according to your own muscular structure, what suits you best to grasp the perception of the second inhaling stage (Gills/Intercostal) of Conditioned Breathing by choosing to bring your arms up on the inhale in one of the following:

- Below your shoulders.
- At your shoulder level.
- Above your shoulders by your head.

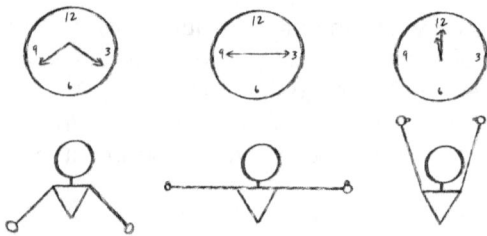

*Figure 5.11* Arm positions for inhaling.

### Kinesthetic Diaphragm Experiment: The Piston

1) Lay on your back with your knees up to the ceiling, the width of your hips apart and the soles of your feet resting on the ground. Interlock your hands on your solar plexus.
2) Inhale on the usual six counts pattern of the previous experiments. Keep your fingers interlocked on your sternum. Do not use force or over-stretch. Simply lengthen your arms with your palms facing down towards your low abdomen.
3) Exhale over nine counts with tempered breath on "s" at 40% and News, allowing your arms to return to their original position. Then repeat.

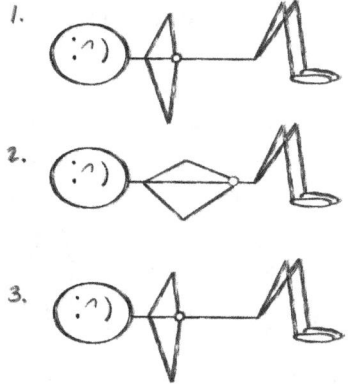

*Figure 5.12* The three positions for the Piston.

Variation #1:

1) Everything remains the same but this time during your inhale, your arms, with hands interlocked, will move away parallel towards your knees at a 45° angle. Shoulders do not leave the floor. Arms lengthen.
2) During the nine counts of the exhale, you will unlock the hands and follow the natural motion of the arms, lengthening, towards landing on the floor. Once the arms reach the floor, begin taking your forearms towards your sternum and end up with your hands interlocked again by Count 9.

You are now ready to repeat the experiment again.

To close this section on breath, let me leave you with the words of infamous Persian poet and Sufi mystic Rumi. Allow Rumi's words to permeate your imagination.

> *"There is one way of breathing that is shameful and constricted. Then, there's another way: a breath of love that takes you all the way to infinity."*
>
> – Rumi

## Alignment

It is important that the voice lives in a body where the skeletal and muscular forces are properly distributed and aligned. Verticality encourages muscle tonicity and relieves constriction of the body and throat.

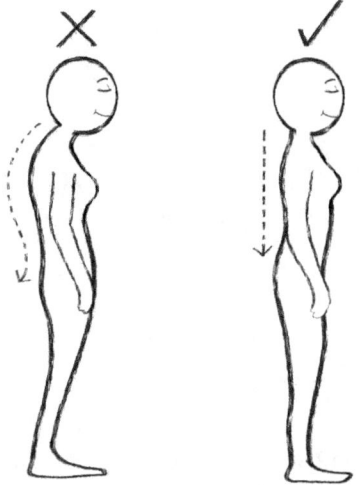

*Figure 5.13* Proper alignment of the spine.

There are many different terms to describe a "neutral body position." In the Barrantes Voice System, I call it the **Relative Position** because individuals are different in their own constitution. Fundamentally, we are talking of a parallel second ballet position with subtle variations.

When the feet, pelvis, torso, and skull are aligned on top of one another, the movement of the body can come freely from the core. This adds efficiency to body mechanics and major system functions, by distributing skeletal and muscular forces evenly throughout the whole body.

When we achieve spinal verticality, the fight against gravity diminishes and muscular tonicity improves. When the torso is straight, the thorax can expand. The head rests on the shoulders and the throat is available to produce sound without force or stress.

This alignment creates a chain reaction in the body which transmits even to the inner ear where our sense of balance resides, allowing us to ground and center ourselves in the space we will be working.

**Lengthen spine----> all along the body ---->**
**inner ear ----> muscular tone ----> free larynx**

Good alignment of the body augments the cortical stimulation of the parietal lobes of the brain (the occiput, or the back of your head). Elements like visual perception and attention, proprioception, and language-processing information take place in this area of the brain.

Proper alignment helps to also integrate several sensorial body functions. This is extremely relevant for the actor given the actor's relationship to language, space, and how to optimize them both for the stage.

### The Relative Position

The "Relative Position" is a very useful stance for starting and finishing the experiments you implement in the training.

1) The feet play a crucial part in this alignment. Weight should be evenly distributed between the toes, metatarsals, and heels. For those with a virtually non-existent arch, think of distributing your weight by imagining a scalene triangle (a triangle with three unequal sides) linking the big toe, pinky, and middle of your heel together.

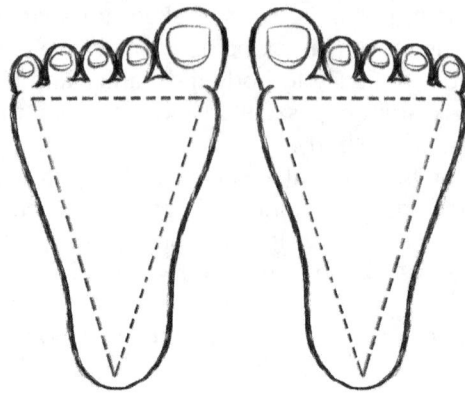

*Figure 5.14* Relative Position feet placement.

If your feet were soup bowls, the soup should be even between the front, middle and back of your dish (your feet).

*Figure 5.15* Think of the bowls as your feet so the toes, the metatarsals, and the heels are evenly distributed.

2) Place your feet parallel with the width of one of your own feet in between. Spine lengthened. Soft knees. Bring your right heel and place it perpendicularly to your left big toe. Then lift up and pivot your right foot around the axe of your right bunion (first joint of the big toe). Your feet will end up being parallel to the width of your hips.

Alternatively, you can arrive at the same stance by doing first ballet position: heels together and toes apart at a 90° angle. Lift up the toes of both feet and pivot your feet around each bunion so that you end in second position with feet parallel.

3) Soften your knees slightly. Soft knees will keep you engaged at all times with the energy and weight of your pelvis. Align your

kneecaps within the "corridor" space between your big toes and pinkies. Visualize connecting the middle of the patella (kneecap) with the center of the hip joint. Hip sockets over and above your heels. Shoulders over hip sockets. Have your spine lengthened, as if you had pneumatic bubbles in between each vertebra. Comb your hair upwards to lengthen the cervical spine. Make sure that you maintain your weight distributed evenly on the ensemble of the foot, paying particular attention to the outside of your feet.

Your weight and skeletal forces should be now evenly distributed. Your alignment, now being in place, makes your trachea and esophagus lengthened, allowing you to optimize your sound production.

## Shower Mouth

Remember the French popular saying related to Shower Mouth: *être bouche bée* (see page 43). This is one of the very first notions I introduce in my teaching, as it is essential for attaining the healthiest possible voice production.

Imagine a shower and its showerhead at a 45° angle, spurting water onto your head and forehead. Notice what happens to the jaw: it drops, it relaxes, and it hangs loose so that water does not suffocate us by entering the nostrils.

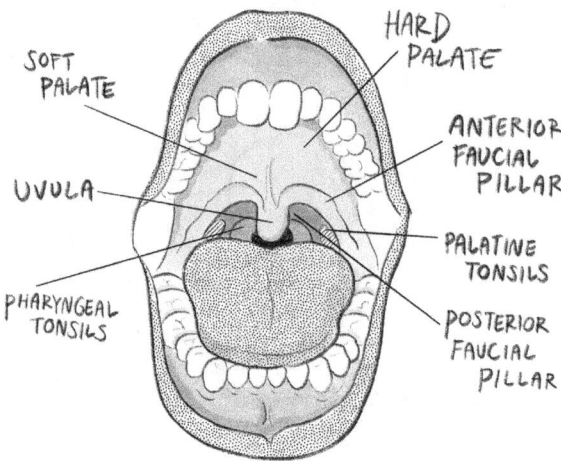

*Figure 5.16* Anatomy of the mouth.

The *Shower Mouth* is a totally natural, vertical drop of the jaw. Images like a silo, a tall vertical door, or the mouth of a horse, a hippopotamus or a crocodile convey that same verticality. It is essential to encourage this vertical gesture of the jaw because it facilitates the traveling path of the sound minimizing obstacles, like tightness of the jaw or the hurdle of the tongue.

The jaw should remain supple and relaxed during phonation because the jaw participates in the pronunciation of words[2] facilitating the laryngeal descent and increasing the size of the resonators.

This is the type of mouth you want to have when producing sound because it comes from a place of pure relaxation and a lack of effort. It is never about consciously opening your mouth or jaw to produce sound, but about making sure that the sound follows the easiest passage to reach the listener. As you encourage this natural gesture, make sure you avoid any pursing of the lips or the tendency to create a "smile." This is a completely vertical gesture. There is nothing horizontal about it.

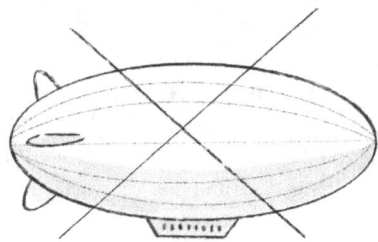

*Figure 5.17* A blimp, a horizontal shape, is undesirable for voice production.

*Figure 5.18* The silo, a vertical shape, is desirable for voice production.

## Duhhhh Experiment

1) Use *Shower Mouth* and produce the sound "Duhhhh" on your natural pitch on each of the following steps.
2) First place your tongue between your teeth, then through the teeth (as if showing the tip of your tongue). Feel the connection with your diaphragm.
3) Next, pass the lips with your tongue, as if letting it hang out of your mouth without force.
4) To end, repeat step one as you started with your tongue between your teeth. This will allow your temporomandibular joint (TMJ), which connects the mandible to the skull, to be unrestricted and supple.

## Shower Mouth *Shakes Experiment*

I prefer this experiment to what other voice methodologies do, which is to grab the lower jaw with the thumb and index fingers and shake it up and down.

1) Hold both hands softly in front of you keeping the arms and armpits open. Have your legs plié in second position and keep your pelvis aligned with your Dantien active. Give small vibratory shakes to the hands and arms, thus encouraging the jaw to flop and dangle with ease and abandon. Use the "NGA-A-A-A" sound when you do this.

## Scaffolding and Monitoring of the Shower Mouth *Experiment*

To create body memory for *Shower Mouth*, I suggest the following to ensure that the jaw remains in the optimal position.

*Figure 5.19* "L" shape scaffold and fingers on Adam's apple monitoring Shower Mouth.

The cervical belt is lengthened, so "comb" the hair upwards. Allow the *Shower Mouth* to appear and let it stay there while doing the following:

1) Make an "L" shape with your right-hand thumb and index fingers. The index finger should be on the middle of the chin at the "dimple" spot, while the thumb should rest on the right clavicle collarbone of the right shoulder. This creates what I call a "scaffold" that helps guarantee that your jaw will not close as soon as sound is produced.
2) With your other hand, rest the left index and middle fingers on the larynx, exactly where the Adam's apple and thyroid cartilage is. The tip of the tongue should rest behind the lower incisors. Use "NGA" sound, staccato, legato, and oscillating it as a sine wave.
3) Do the following actions several times:

    a. Swallow in slow motion (the larynx comes up before it goes down).
    b. Yawn in slow motion.

Notice that in both actions the larynx goes down. It is important and beneficial to have an elastic larynx that can easily descend without employing effort.

### Role of the Shower Mouth on Tongue #3

One of the key elements for voice work is to have a free jaw and a free tongue so that sound can pass through without obstacles and effort. Tongue 3 (see page 112) is ideal for this, but in order to attain it, please follow the following exercise:

Maintain *Shower Mouth*, with the tip of the tongue behind the lower incisors. Imagine having just placed a small hot potato in your mouth. Since it is HOT, and to burn the mouth as little as possible, it is necessary to create space in one of two ways:

1) Create space above the "hot potato" by naturally lifting the soft palate.
2) Create space around and below the potato by allowing the larynx to descend. Release the air to cool the back of the tongue, where the potato first landed.

### Gills and Intercostal Awakening

Throughout my years of teaching, I have often referred to the Intercostal muscle system as the "Gills." Considering your Gills in connection with your diaphragm as part of your training is critical for strengthening your voice.

Visualize this area as the gills of a large fish, as the motion of opening and closing of an accordion, as bellows, or two large fans on each side of your torso.

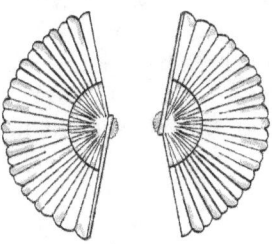

*Figure 5.20* Two fans as inhaling Gills.

### Gills Fanning Out Experiment

Sit on the floor in the tailor position. Left leg is crossed in front. Relax. Allow your torso to collapse along with all your biographical idiosyncrasies. Arms by your side.

Exhale, inhale, exhale, and get ready for final inhale before the experiment starts. Apply Conditioned Breathing for the experiment. Execute the experiment with tempered breath at 40%. Drive the work by image (News). When you inhale, remain still.

Fiction energy is present everywhere in your body and your biography has been eclipsed by this point. The arm motion should be synchronized with the duration of your exhale.

Begin first with the right side of your torso:

1) Inhale at ease, Inner Tube/Buddha Belly.

*Figure 5.21* Position 1 of Gills Fanning Out.

2) As you exhale, temper the breath with a hissing "s" at 40%. Allow the spine to lengthen, vertebrae by vertebrae, for the entire duration of the breath without effort as if you were slowly hoisting a sail. Your arms move out to each side to the inverted 10:10 form with your fingertips gently flaring the floor.

*Figure 5.22* Position 2 of Gills Fanning Out.

3) Inhale calmly in the position you first arrived with Buddha Belly/Inner Tube. On the next exhale, the right arm goes steadily up, as if to touch the right intersection between the ceiling and the wall at 45°.

*Figure 5.23* Position 3 of Gills Fanning Out.

4) Inhale calmly in the position you arrived. On the next exhale, the right arm should become perpendicular to the ceiling, fully lengthened without locking it. Your scapulae should be connected down to your back and shoulders.

*Figure 5.24* Position 4 of Gills Fanning Out.

5) Inhale calmly in the position you arrived. On the next exhale, the right arm should go up steadily, as if to touch this time the left intersection between the ceiling and the wall (45°) of the room. Your left arm, slightly flexed, supports your weight. Notice how your right gill (Intercostal muscles) expands.

*Figure 5.25* Position 5 of Gills Fanning Out.

## 104 The Industry of Breath and Alignment

6) Inhale calmly in the position you arrived. On the next exhale, the left elbow is going to drop gently to the floor (this may take practice) and with no force like a Rolls Royce's car shock absorber. Maintain your right arm lengthened upwards to balance the weight of your torso. Do not over-stretch sideways.

Exhale in this position so that you stretch a little further, perhaps even no more than 1/8 inch. The fingertips are very active, as if they were laser beams or search lights giving light into sky. Inhale calmly in this position.

*Figure 5.26* Position 6 of Gills Fanning Out.

7) "Windshield Wiper and Around the World:" This exhale is going to be the longest exhale you make. It should be synchronized with two main actions during it. First action of the exhale: the right arm should come down passing in front of your face while moving towards the floor, like the movement of a car's windshield wiper. The body is working on two-dimensional 90° planes – one horizontal/the pelvis, and the other vertical/the torso.

*Figure 5.27* Position 7 of Gills Fanning Out.

8) Second action of the exhale: As the fingertips of the right hand touch the ground, then allow the right shoulder and the torso

to follow the motion that the right arm is going to execute as you maintain your sitz bones on the floor.

*Figure 5.28* Position 8 of Gills Fanning Out.

9) Draw a wide semicircle (180°) from left to right as your fingertips flair the floor as if you were drawing the line of the equator, going "around the world."

*Figure 5.29* Position 9 of Gills Fanning Out.

10) As your right arm reaches your right-hand side, inhale calmly and bring the knees up together.

*Figure 5.30* Position 10 of Gills Fanning Out.

11) Exhale with a most comfortable sigh while the legs stretch out to your sides at 90°, to the inverted 10:10 position.

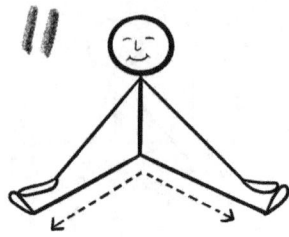

*Figure 5.31* Position 11 of Gills Fanning Out.

Close your eyes and take a few seconds to assess the work you have completed. Proceed to do the experiment again but on the opposite side.

### Sargasso Torso Experiment

1) Take the Relative Position 2 feet away facing a wall. Rest the length of your arms above your head with your palms flat on the wall. Take small steps away from the wall as you begin to undulate and ripple your spine, gently, softly, with no effort.
2) After a minute or so you should end up creating a perfect 90° tabletop shape with your arms lengthened and supporting your torso on the wall, while your spine is horizontal and parallel to the floor. Your legs should be soft and gently flexed to allow the small constant swaying, rippling motion to take place. No force should be applied. Only allow gentle undulations. Initiate the movement from the tailbone to the top of the spine. Always very tentatively. The smaller the movement, the deeper the muscular work takes place.
3) To finish the experiment, make sure you reverse the steps: walking slowly back towards the wall without losing this supple seaweed motion of your spine.

## Imagery

- Long sargasso seaweed floating, swaying, rippling, undulating with soft supple, nimble, willowy movements in a calm sea.

## Gills on Horse Experiment

Conditioned Breathing on tempered breath, "NG" and "NGA" on your natural pitch.

1) Inhale on six counts:

Start in second plié position. Start with your hands clasped in front of your sternum.

*Figure 5.32* Inhaling positions 1–6 of the Gills on Horse.

- Counts 1–2–3: through the nose/abdomen as your hands, clasped, they turn down finishing with your arms lengthened by your low abdomen.
- Counts 4–5–6: with Shower Mouth/Gills) as your arms move forward and upwards towards until they reach the level of your sternum by the sixth count.

2) Exhale on nine counts:

*Figure 5.33* Repeat the sequence 1–9 on the exhale of the Gills on Horse.

- Counts 1–2–3: unclasp your hands allowing your arms to move out to your sides, at your sternum level, until they reach an inverted 10:10 parallel to the floor. Lead this movement with your wrists out and open but without using force.
- Counts 4–5–6: with your arms still lengthened, allow them to come down 45° away from your sides, pointing diagonally down to the floor.
- Counts 7–8–9: use these last three counts to allow the hands to meet, by the low abdomen, then clasp the fingers and allow the hands to move up until they finish facing the sternum by Count 9.

3) You have reached again your starting position. Repeat the sequence several times.

## Tabletop Against the Wall Experiment

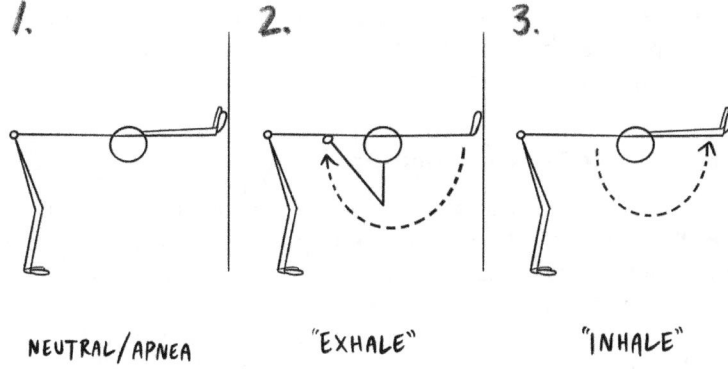

Figure 5.34 Positions 1–3 (Neutral, Exhale, and Inhale) of Tabletop Against the Wall.

1) Create a tabletop with your torso so that a friend can rest their breakfast tray on your flat back to have it in peace. Lean your torso forward with soft stretched arms supporting your torso against the wall. Your spine is lengthened, flat and parallel to the ceiling and floor at a 90° angle in relation to your pelvis. Maintain soft knees.
2) Inhale on six counts:

    - Counts 1–2–3: through the nose/abdomen connection.
    - Counts 4–5–6: through Shower Mouth/Gills.

3) Exhale on nine counts:

    - Counts 1–9: your right arm sweeps gently towards the floor ending up by your opposite hip as it torques your upper part of the torso simultaneously.

4) Inhale on six counts:

    - Counts 1–6: allow the arm to come back to the previous staring position.

# 110  The Industry of Breath and Alignment

5) Exhale on nine counts:

- Counts 1–9: your left arm sweeps gently towards the floor ending up by your opposite hip as it torques your upper part of the torso simultaneously.

## Three Basic Tongue Positions

A flexible voice is essential for all stage work. For this to happen the larynx should be able to drop into the throat so that as performers we can provide our audiences with optimum expressivity, strength, and vocal connection.

The tongue is implicated in this capability for the larynx to descend. A free, loose jaw and tongue helps sound to travel without unnecessary effort, finding clear and resonant passages. To implement and experience the mobility of the larynx and optimize voice flexibility, I consider three basic tongue positions.

*Figure 5.35* The three basic tongue positions represented as: a front yard, a home interior, and a back yard.

Practice the following tongue positions often to create body memory and technique.

## Tongue #1: Front Yard

*Figure 5.36* A front yard as Tongue #1.

Shower Mouth. Placing the tip of your tongue behind the lower incisors, fold the tongue "out" of the mouth (imagine creating a wave). Allow space between the back of the tongue and the upper incisors. Because you are in Shower Mouth, the jaw drop is exclusively vertical.

Make sure you do not "add" lip tension (pursing) or a smile. Keep it pure and simple.

Notice how the larynx elevates and comes up.

### Imagery

- Cannoli.
- Spring roll.
- A wave just about to spill forward like a rolling pin.

*Figure 5.37* A wave spilling over as a rolling pin in the ocean for Tongue #1.

## Tongue #2: Home

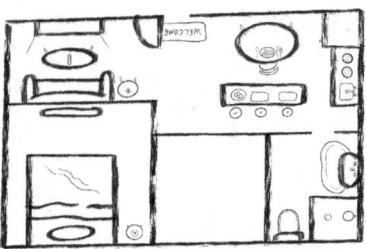

*Figure 5.38* The interior of a home as Tongue #2.

Shower Mouth. Relax the tongue fully from Tongue #1 back into the natural base of the mouth where it belongs. The tip of the tongue should be behind and in contact with the lower incisors. Allow the tongue to rest comfortably "in its bed," "in its home," doing nothing. Tongue #2 is pedestrian, ordinary, daily, and simply rests where it belongs.

Unless you allow it to rest flat in the jaw's frame, the tongue will become an obstacle. It has to be free of tension, soft and relaxed, like the bottom sheet of a fresh new bed.

Notice how the larynx comes down from position.

### Imagery

- Flattened pastry dough.
- An unrolled yoga mat.
- The bottom sheet of a fresh new bed.
- The tongue is lying down having a "siesta."

## Tongue #3: Back Yard

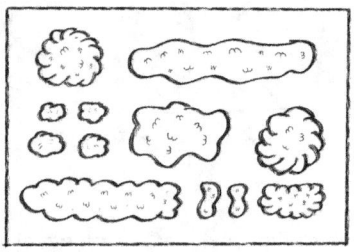

*Figure 5.39* Bushes in a back yard as Tongue #3.

The key element with this tongue position is that you want two simultaneous, opposite, but complementary actions to take place.

One is that the soft palate lifts as the root of the tongue drops down simultaneously into the larynx. The combination of these two actions engages the mouth muscles and soft palate pillars in the best way to optimize voice production.

On Shower Mouth, with the tip of the tongue behind the lower incisors, imagine placing a small hot potato in your mouth. Since you do not want to burn your mouth, you want to minimize the contact of the hot potato in your mouth. To cool off the hot potato and the space around it, you will exhale short puffs of breath, lifting simultaneously your soft palate high up in your mouth, as if you were opening a large sports umbrella, yawning, or creating a large dome in your mouth.

There are two ways to do this at the same time:

- Creating space above the potato by naturally lifting a soft veil. Imagine yawning or how a large sport umbrella opens.
- Creating space around and below the potato. Allow the larynx to descend as air is released, "cooling" the back of the tongue. Make sure to produce an aspirated "HA" sound, either in percussive or sustained form, on the exhale. This sound should mimic the sound of a panting dog.

Notice how this action, which takes place in the oro- and laryngopharynx, makes your larynx descend and thus creates the potential for a large, hollow, open, resonant chamber.

### *Imagery*

- Individuality and personality of a back yard.
- Hot potato/umbrella.
- The domes of the Taj Mahal, the Hagia Sophia, Pantheon, Vatican, etc.
- The half dome of the Hollywood Bowl.
- The 360° dome of a planetarium.

*Figure 5.40* Taj Mahal as Tongue #3.

*Figure 5.41* Pantheon as Tongue #3.

*Figure 5.42* Hagia Sophia as Tongue #3.

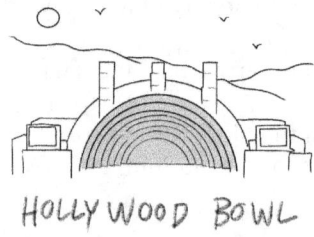

*Figure 5.43* Hollywood Bowl as Tongue #3.

## Cornerstones

- Your neck should be lengthened without the use of force. "Comb" your hair upwards and imagine pneumatic air bubbles like in a spirit level.
- Shower Mouth always.
- Monitor your work by "scaffolding"[3] your Shower Mouth.
- Make sure that in all three tongue positions the tip of the tongue remains in contact with the lower incisors.
- There is a tendency to naturally retract the tongue without even realizing it – look at yourself in a mirror if necessary.
- Use your natural pitch at 40% on "NG" and "NGA," in legato/staccato modes.

## Da Pacem Cordium Experiment

Sing the whole of "Da Pacem Cordium" chant on each of the three tongue vocal textures and combine it either with improvised or proverbial physical expression.

Variation on Holding Tongue Position #1:

Produce the same quality sounds you did in Tongues #1, #2, and #3 but this time only using and maintaining physically the position of Tongue #1. While you make the sound of Tongue #2 and #3, the muscular focus will be on the palatine arches and the pillars of the faucial pillars.

I recommend you observe yourself in a mirror to make sure you do not change the position of the Tongue #1 until you build enough body memory to do it without it.

## Horizontal/Transversal Placement Perception of Tongue #1, #2, #3 Experiment

The only difference with the previous basic tongue experiment is that in this variation you want to "move the sound transversally" doing the three basic tongue positions. Do this three times through (front–middle–back, back–middle–front, front–middle–back) as you sustain the sound using only one breath.

Visualize horizontally and transversally how the sound moves from the front yard (front of your mouth, oral cavity) to the back yard (cervical vertebrae, oropharynx).

### Imagery

- From the forward curling of Tongue #1, to the flattening of Tongue #2, think of it as if you were unrolling a carpet or flattening dough with a rolling pin.
- As you move into Tongue #3 use the image of hot potato/umbrella.

### Cornerstones

- "Scaffold" – Shower Mouth using natural pitch at 40%.
- The tip of your tongue is always behind the lower incisors on all three tongues.
- Use Conditioned Breathing inhaling on six counts and exhaling on nine.

### Effects

- A larger space in the nasopharynx, oropharynx, and laryngopharynx, which increases acoustic resonance.
- Strengthens your soft palate and larynx musculature.

### Matterhorn-Cervino Tongue Experiment

Use your natural pitch this time and have your Shower Mouth closed with your lips resting on each other without any tension.

1) Take six counts to breath in as you draw simultaneously the tip of the tongue from behind the low incisors up to end up on the sixth count at the threshold between the hard and soft palate as if you just created a mountain top like the Matterhorn.

MOUNT CERVINO

*Figure 5.44* Tip of the tongue represented by Mount Cervino to help differentiate the soft and hard palate.

2) Allow the tongue to remain in this pointy shape for the next nine exhaling counts.
3) Visualize allowing the larynx to descend further down during the exhalation without using force. At the end of the nine-exhale count allow the tongue to return to starting position and repeat.

After doing the experiment three or four times notice:

- The larger space generated both in the mouth as well as in the larynx.
- If the quality or the pitch of your natural pitch has modified.

## Cornerstones

- "Scaffold" your Shower Mouth.
- Do the experiment using both: only breath but also "NG" vocalization.
- The tip of your tongue is in the middle of your mouth, at the threshold between the hard and soft palate.
- Use Conditioned Breathing inhaling on six counts and exhaling on nine.

## Support of Sound with Diaphragm

### *Process and Stages*

Phase I

> Body and sound bounces. Start in the Relative Position by first bouncing and humming (8 beats, 20%). Stop humming and utter "NG-A" on Tongue #3 at 40%. The pelvic floor should feel gravid, with ease. Your natural pitch will fluctuate around one to one-and-a-half tones. Visualize the image of a sine wave monitoring one's heart rate.

Phase II

> Execute only vocal production without physical bouncing. You are still with your feet grounded. The same experiment as in Phase I but without the support of the body. Imagine as if you were doing an audio recording of the previous Phase I rather than a video.

Phase III

> Employ body and sound again to ease the work. Allow your body to go down–up–down–up–down–up–down and stay down and sustain the note as you stop bouncing. The Pelvis is aligned and centered. The spine is lengthened.

Phase IV

> Only vocal production. The same experiment as in Phase III but without the support of the body. Imagine doing an audio recording of the previous Phase III.

Phase V

> Frisbee throw. Body and sound together. Use only the arm to throw. Nothing else moves in the body. Hand at navel level. Maintain the length of the spine (avoid tilting the torso and flamingo/guillotine neck). Your front leg is bent while your back leg is lengthened, grounding your weight.
> The moment the imaginary frisbee is released with impulsive passion ("schhhlack" percussive sound) is the moment the natural pitch sound starts on "NGA." Sustain it until breathing amber light tells you to suspend the sound.

Phase VI

> Only vocal production. The same as in previous Phase V but without the support of the body. Imagine as if you were doing a recording of Phase V. As if a singing member of a choir.

Phase VII

> Body and sound together. I refer to it as "Broadway 7."
> Start from your Relative Position, in one sudden movement create an open five-point star gesture: legs at 10:10, on a second "plié" with open arms at an inverted 10:10 position, fingertips with energy, the spine is lengthened. Pelvis aligned and centered with confidence. Your whole body is expansive, joyous, and slightly on Broadway presentational attitude.
> The entire body is in a tonic state. Avoid tension. Imagine as if five dishes are being released from the hands, feet, and from

behind the neck (occipital). This action should evoke the energy released in clay shooting pigeons sports.

Phase VIII

Body and sound. "Off Broadway."

The same as in the previous Phase VII but moving in space freely for 30 seconds at a time. Breathe as often as necessary. Feel free to change notes as long as you do it with ease. Move constantly with Fiction and News and shift the tempo freely as long as the sound does not become the wobbly, relaxed sound you did on the very Phase I. Avoid playing it safe, take risks. Evaluate the diaphragm's use and tonicity in the body.

## Cornerstones

- Use Natural Pitch – once you begin to use 40% make sure that you use this intensity all along.
- Shower Mouth, tip of the tongue behind the lower incisors.
- Head, torso, and pelvis bounce in one piece.
- Use Fiction and News in all the eight phases.

## Lip Trills

**Lip trills** are a very useful and effective warm up. Start on your Natural Pitch and then move half tone by half tone up and down the scale. A lip trill should sound like a motor engine. Young children make this sound often to illustrate cars or motorbikes in motion. Use sound: "BRRRRRR."

If the lips do not manage to flutter at ease, place the thumb and index finger on the corners of your lips as if to bring them forward gently. This should relax any chronic lip tension.

Lip trills are an efficient vocal exercise because they help calibrate the ratio of air pressure and pitch while maintaining a relaxed larynx. More importantly, they balance the pressure above and below the vocal cords, smoothing the transition between the traditional denominations of "head" and "chest" voice registers.

Make sure to maintain the *same intensity of sound* without expending extra effort. Be wary of increasing the intensity as you go up in pitch. Notice how the diaphragm is "tonic" while doing this (40% intensity). As the pitch rises in a *glissando*, think of the notes as if you were coming down and vice versa.

This experiment narrows the glottal passage where air exits the throat, which in turn slows down the airflow and involves the diaphragm. Lip trills offer optimal collaboration between the diaphragm and the vocal apparatus because to produce this sound, the vocal folds and muscles must be relaxed.

### *Lip Trills Experiment – Pitch*

As you do the lip trills, focus on shifting your pitch:

- Bouncing 4 x 8 on natural pitch.
- Bouncing 4 x 8 from natural pitch, going up on a glissando up the octave.
- Bouncing 4 x 8 from the octave, going down on a glissando back to your natural pitch.

### *Lip Trills Experiment – Movement*

As you do the lip trills, focus on your body movement:

1) Move the head right/left for as long as the breath feels comfortable sustaining sound.
2) Move the head right/left for as long as the breath feels comfortable using Shomio pattern's sequences (see further details under the section *Voice Like Concrete: Shomio*).
3) Move the head right/left for as long as the breath feels comfortable doing **Nancy's Boots** (see further details under the section *Voice Like Concrete: Shomio*).
4) Move the head right/left for as long as the breath feels comfortable doing 2001 (see further details under the section *Voice Like Concrete: Shomio*).

### **Four Times Eight**

The following experiment, simple as it is, is crucial for your daily warm up and voice maintenance.

Starting from the Relative Position, bounce 32 times on each of the three tongues using natural pitch at 40%. This is really a dynamic progression in space of the Phase 1 of "Support of Sound with Diaphragm." Feel the **gravidness** of the pelvis and the support of the pelvic floor.

The merging of sound and body support should be blatant. Inhale just before the first count of each series of eight bounces. Make sure that you only move with each first step and that you step with the entire foot (toes, metatarsals, and heel) at the same time, using the same amount of pressure on each of the three areas of the foot. Use small steps so that you do not lose your alignment. Get comfortable but heavy, and have your knees soft by bouncing lightly, never straightening them.

Avoid the tendency for the eyes to glaze over. The gaze should be focused with News and never vacant. You also want to avoid any rocking forwards or backwards of the pelvis as you bounce your weight. Head, torso, and pelvis move synergically in one piece.

When you arrive to Tongue Position #3, tap the back of the neck for the first 16 counts. Tap lightly enough to encourage the flow of blood in this cervical area. This will help you to locate how far back the sound should be coming from.

Imagine an acoustic or visual **sine wave** of a heart rate monitor.

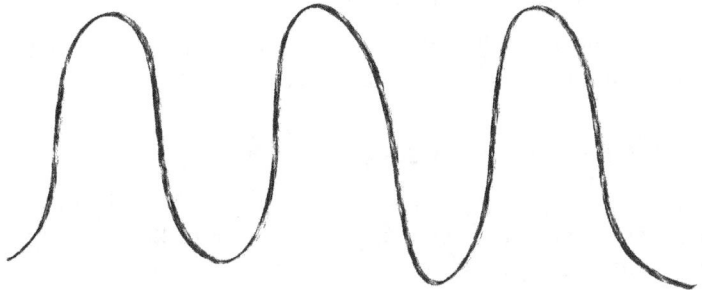

*Figure 5.45* Visual sine wave of a heart rate monitor.

The weight you experience should feel like lifting a heavy-duty plastic bag with water. Try to imagine that your body's gravity center is as low as in being several months pregnant.

## 4 x 8 Experiment

1) Do a cycle three times (32 counts/bounces) on your natural pitch at 40% on NGA.
2) Start with 32 counts/bounces on your natural pitch; then do another 32 counts/bounces on the fifth and finish the cycle with 32 counts/bounces on the octave.
3) Do another cycle, but this time reverse the interval progression. In other words, start on the octave, then the fifth and finish the last 32 counts/bounces on your natural pitch.

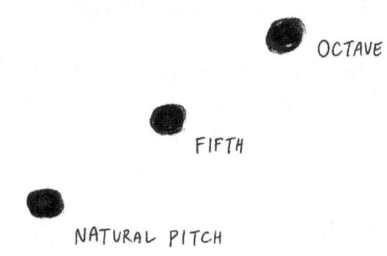

*Figure 5.46* Visual representation of Natural Pitch, the Fifth, and its Octave.

## 4 x 8 Experiment with Tongues

The same as you did in the previous Variation #1 but using this time a different tongue for each cycle.

## 4 x 8 Experiment with Song

Find a favorite song of yours to which you can fit eight counts/bounces. Choose to accentuate certain beat or beats within the eight counts at your discretion. Feel free to change accents every cycle or every couple of cycles. Use all three tongues with "NG" and "NGA." Change tongues every couple of cycles.

## 4 x 8 Experiment with Going Up and Down the Scale

Starting on your natural pitch with "NGA" at 40%, do eight counts/bounces half step by half step per note going up the scale until you reach the fifth, or the octave if you feel comfortable enough. Help yourself by playing each of the half step notes that you will be singing every eight counts on the piano or keyboard. Once you reach the fifth or the octave, come down the scale half step by half step always on eight counts/bounces until you reach your natural pitch.

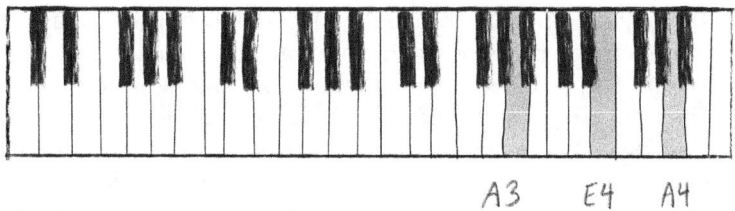

*Figure 5.47* Piano keys showing A3, E4, and A4.

## Voice Like Concrete: Shomio

Unearthing the trove of treasures of the multi-octave vocal range requires similar nurturing, patience, and rigor as the field of archaeology does when recovering human material in excavations.

Remember that you are building your voice, an instrument inside you that must face the unnatural needs that the stage imposes upon the actor. As a result, the vocal muscles must be resilient.

When thinking about working on new areas of the voice, approach it as if you were building with concrete. A self-respected builder will strive to use only the perfect mixture of gravel, sand, cement, and water. When building with concrete, the new layer is only poured *after the first layer has matured and settled.*

For the concrete's filler and binder to consolidate properly, multiple elements must be considered: stiffening time, volume, surface, density, temperature, composition, etc. Only the right dosage and combination of each of these elements will consolidate the material, making it strong and effective for years to come.

While the process can be physically seen and tested when building with concrete, the same cannot be said when working with the voice. Once the voice-body becomes strained while hitting a particular note, it is important to spend extra time working out the kinks in order to create a strong foundation when vocalizing up or down successive notes of the scale.

*Spending time on a particular troublesome note* (think about pouring in the second layer of concrete) *will facilitate the transition to the next note.* It also allows the voice to "settle into the saddle," getting firmly grounded. If this principle is observed, the voice will not be stressed or damaged.

The objective in voice production is for the larynx to remain as low in the pharynx as possible. This way, it remains available to sound and is produced with minimum effort and tension.

The daily voice of the performer has inevitable thresholds. If producing a sound requires too much effort or induces strain, check in with yourself, monitor and review where the pitch of your range is; stay longer on the note below the one that caused strain and ask your teacher for guidance, if necessary, but your own observation is the key.

Remember: it is essential to *be patient while you earn* certain difficult notes on your range or on a particular voice texture.

Do not be afraid to spend a few weeks or even months on one particular note or texture of your voice. You have so many years ahead for sustaining your career once you have built your foundation. Allow time for your voice to settle into your body and experience.

### Shomio

I regularly use the following vocal experiment to center, develop, and maintain the voice. It is inspired by Japanese Shomio Buddhist chanting, which is primarily used in the Tendai and Shingon traditions and has existed for hundreds of years. This type of chant originated in India. It employs a pentatonic scale and uses an interesting progression of semitones in its melodic lines. This form of chanting has inspired me to develop the performer's elemental voice by tempering the diaphragm while strengthening, supporting, and controlling the breath. It also helps to develop one's vocal range while maintaining the larynx in a low position with Tongue Position #3.

Vocalization is done on your Natural Pitch sustaining one long "NGA" for a total of 24 beats, maintaining the sound in Tongue #3 at 40% throughout the experiment. In class I tend to use B3;

however, when you do this on your own, please use your own natural pitch.

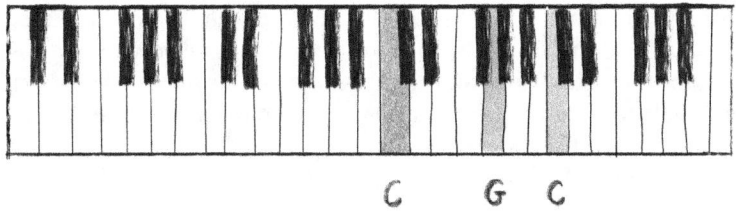

*Figure 5.48* Piano keys showing C, G, and C.

### Shomio on the Fifth Experiment

1) **Four beats.** Start with the body in Relative Position. Inhale on easy six counts. As you exhale, bend the knees, and sustain "NGA" on our natural pitch for four counts. Make sure the tongue is in Back Yard position (Tongue #3).
2) **Eight beats.** Bounce on each beat for eight counts. Begin a "sine wave/bird fluttering" sound interval on your natural pitch. Each first beat is on natural pitch while the second one is a 1/3 above. On beat 16 move to the fifth above your natural pitch.
3) **Eight beats.** Maintain 40% intensity and from that fifth note begin a slow, downwards glissando until you reach your original natural pitch. As you do the downward glissando, visualize the image of a skier doing a ski-flying jump.
4) **Four beats.** As you land on the snow, ground, and sustain your natural pitch for four beats.

Variation #1:

The same rhythmic structure of *Shomio on the 5th* but now using the following intervals:

- Shomio on the octave.
- Shomio on the octave and a third.
- Shomio on the octave and a half.

### Nancy's Boots Experiment

The title of this Shomio variation, **Nancy's Boots**, is based on Nancy Sinatra's song "These Boots are Made for Walking," because we are going to focus on vocalizing a downward glissando mimicking the famous bass line of the song. We use the intervals to tune our voices and achieve musical accuracy, combining it with playfulness.

In this experiment we are going to use:

- Shower Mouth with Tongue #3, "Back Yard."
- Start on your Natural Pitch at 40%.
- *Broadway 7* body position (for proper position, see Figure 6.9).

The structure is like the Shomio experiment except that we will add 12 extra beats and we will cover a full octave range. Notice that every time we change notes, we vocalize the "NGA" sound to give us extra support with the diaphragm.

1) Starting at your natural pitch, move up the scale progressively, half tone by half tone, until you encounter the first bridge. Make sure there is no strain in your voice or body.
2) For body support we will use Broadway 7 throughout the entire vocalization. Complete the experiment properly before starting again. Use Fiction, News, and proper body alignment as well as breathing support. Getting out of the experiment:
   a. Bend your torso to the left side, allowing the right arm to become perpendicular to the ceiling
   b. Allow your right leg to join, one foot apart, your left leg while simultaneously your right arm and torso bend down toward your knees. Your torso is going to end in a concave position (like a parenthesis) in relation to the floor.
   c. Unwind slowly your spine until you finish in the same neutral Relative Position as you started. You are ready to start the experiment again.

## 2001 Experiment

1) From your Relative Position move into Broadway 7 in second plié position, arms at an inverted 10:10, spine lengthened. Use Fiction and News. Shower Mouth on Tongue #3 at 40% on your Natural Pitch.

2) Use the following interval:

   - Tonic– fifth– octave starting from your natural pitch and sing four counts on the tonic and the fifth but you will sing the last note for as long as you feel comfortable by acknowledging your natural amber light.

3) Getting out of the experiment:

   - Bend your torso to the left side, allowing the right arm to become perpendicular to the ceiling.
   - Allow your right leg to join, one foot apart, your left leg while simultaneously your right arm and torso bend down toward your knees. Your torso is going to end in a concave position (like a parenthesis) in relation to the floor.
   - Unwind slowly your spine until you finish in the same neutral Relative Position as you started. You are ready to start the experiment again.

## Imagery

- This is the interval Stanley Kubrick used in the iconic film "2001" which comes from the symphonic poem "Also Sprach Zarathustra," composed by Richard Strauss after the philosophical fiction writings of Friedrich Nietzsche.

### Big Ben Bell Strikes Experiment

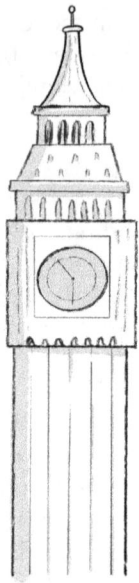

*Figure 5.49* London's Big Ben for centering sound at 40%.

### Preparation

- Use Relative Position and monitor your Shower Mouth through the experiment.
- Produce several panting sounds on Tongue #2 at 20 % (little panting dog image). Notice that your larynx is in the middle of larynx: daily mode.
- Produce several panting sounds on Tongue #3 at 40 % (big panting dog image). Notice that your larynx got lower in your larynx: stage mode.
- Spend 1 minute exploring "NG" and "NGA" in tongues 1–2–3 in different transversal placement progressions.

## Process and Stages

1) Make one long bell sound on "NGA" as if it was the call for attention before striking the hour. Maintain the sound for the duration of your Natural Pitch until your amber light comes up. Breath in.
2) Make four-count long bell sounds on "NGA" as if Big Ben was striking 16:00 p.m. Breathe every time between strikes but remain always on Tongue #3, Back Yard. Breathe in.
3) Make eight short bell sounds on "NGA" as bell (doubling the previous tempo of #2) without changing your Shower Mouth or Tongue #3. Breathe in.
4) Repeat once again the last eight short bell sounds you did on "NGA." Breathe in.
5) Finish the Big Ben bells ringing with four very long bell sounds. Each one of them should be as long as your amber light allows you to do.

## Imagery

- The Big Ben tower joins one's head (clock's face) to one's torso.
- See the clock's face as a 3D sphere in your mouth.
- Feel your mouth as if you had a nice orange in it (hot potato & large sports umbrella).

## Cornerstones

- Natural Pitch at 40% Tongue #3 on your natural pitch on "NGA" all through the experiment. Fiction and News.
- Inhale only through your nose port. Still producing Tongue #3, allow the back of your tongue to move up against your taut soft palate. This forces you to close your mouth port to any in-air.
- Monitor the work. Whether you are inhaling or exhaling your larynx remains low.

## Acoustic Levels

The following acoustic levels are a simplified approach, inspired by cultural anthropologist Edward T. Hall's categorization of space.[4] Hall's four basic criteria – Private, Personal, Social, and

Public – translate into the levels of vocal production needed to activate and manipulate the voice on stage (this classification considers the acoustic space of the voice in relation to the volume of the performance space).

### 1) Private

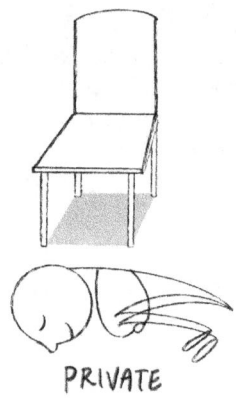

*Figure 5.50* Private/Interior/Self acoustic space.

*Acoustic level:*

0–30% intensity. Translated in musical terms, this vocal quality is called *pianissimo*.

*Supporting Action/Body Source:*

Rest your back on the floor with legs on top of a chair; speak quietly to yourself or as if you were cocooned on the floor.

This quality of sound relates to a specific inner state of being – it is thoughtful, contemplative, and intimate. Think of the vocal decorum that is observed in a library or in a place of worship – think of how people speak when murmuring, telling secrets, or showing respect in a place of remembrance. This voice level can be either voiced or unvoiced.[5] If it is voiced, it is ideal to use it with a microphone, to draw in the listener.

When translated for the stage, The Private becomes what is known as a "stage whisper," an unvoiced form of phonation that does not use laryngeal vibration and is only carried by breath flow. On stage, it also may be used as an "aside" to create a comedic, emphatic effect.

## 2) Personal

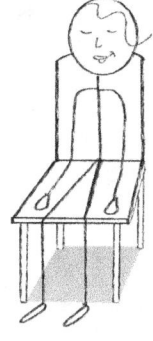

*Figure 5.51* Personal/Soft acoustic space.

*Acoustic level:*

30–45% intensity. Translated into musical terms, this vocal quality is called *piano*.

*Supporting Action/Body Source:*

While sitting on a chair, focus on what is near you. This acoustic space is immediately near to you, a "face to face" space. An individual or individuals entering this acoustic space is indicative of a certain degree of interactive relationship and familiarity.

If related to a group, the intensity of this quality will translate as if we were addressing two to six people maybe at once.

This acoustic level is the most natural and effortless, as it relates to the daily personal space we inhabit during dialogue and exchanges. On stage, however, this level must be *projected*.

### 3) Social

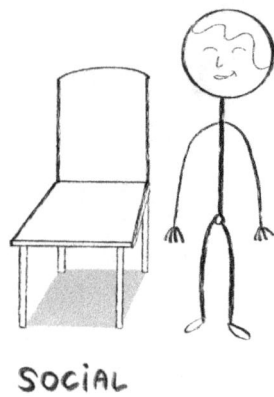

*Figure 5.52* Social/Interactive acoustic space.

*Acoustic level:*

45–60% intensity. Translated into musical terms, this vocal quality is called *forte*.

*Supporting Action/Body Source:*

Stand in front of or next to a chair, as if addressing a large group of people without the use of a microphone.

In ordinary life, this acoustic level would seem overwhelming and imposing. This quality will translate in daily life as if we were addressing a dozen to 20 people at once: a classroom for example. But on stage, this level is completely natural and necessary.

## 4) Public

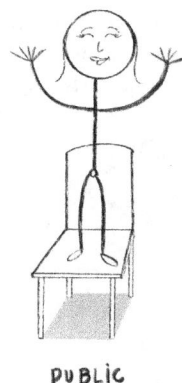

*Figure 5.53* Public/Commanding acoustic space.

*Acoustic level:*

60–70% intensity. Translated into musical terms, this vocal quality is called *fortissimo*.[6]

*Supporting Action/Body Source:*

Stand up on a chair as if addressing a large crowd (forty+ people); normally, this address would require a microphone (imagine a loud voice within a congregation, a political rally, or a sports event, or in an outdoor space such as a busy street, a square, or a park).

Without the assistance of a microphone, this voice level comes across as pompous, loud, and domineering.

However, it is important not to think of this vocal space as one involving screaming; the vocal level is just below shouting.

To this effect, it seems useful to paraphrase Japanese actor Zeami Motokiyo,[7] who suggests that the actor should use 70% vocal intensity while maintaining 100% of the body's inner power.

### Acoustic Coupling

When the column of air and the column of sound overlap perfectly, you end up with a sound that is not only well tuned, but also filled with ample resonance. This is called: **acoustic coupling**.

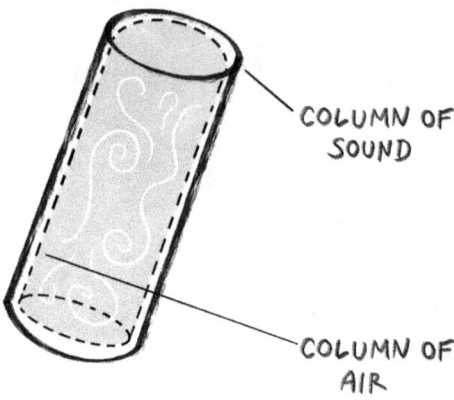

*Figure 5.54* Column representing the optimal flow of sound and air through it to obtain acoustic coupling.

### Imagining Lifting Experiment

When producing a specific note on a certain pitch becomes difficult, you might experience better results and overcome the obstacle by doing the following:

1) Take a second plié position. Align the body. Engage your full body as if you were going to lift a large object (i.e., a piano or a large table), but without soliciting any muscular contraction in the action you are about to execute.
2) Only when your full body is engaged in the action allow your sound or the phrase to come out. It is very important that you do this action without actually lifting or pulling off the floor the heavy object. The key is the muscular engagement not the force or forceful pull of the action.

*Figure 5.55* A person engaging with the weight of a piano for acoustic coupling.

Doing it in this way, you will feel the full tonic muscular engagement of your body muscles. There is no need to use force or contraction of your muscles. It is more of a meshing of your weight with the object than pulling with force or pushing into the object. This helps your diaphragm to support the sound emission as you engage your body with the large object. As a result, your column of air and column of sound "superpose" each other, creating this much desired freeing and gratifying effect of *acoustic coupling*.

## Driving Experiment

1) Sit in your car allowing your weight to fully sink into the seat.
2) With your arms easily lengthened, rest your hands on the driving wheel and very lightly engage your arms as if you were going to get closer to the wheel but without allowing your back to leave the back of your seat. In other words, without letting your body move physically closer to the driving wheel. Notice that we are talking fundamentally of an internal muscular tonifying action that brings along the ensemble of your body and since we are talking about voice production, the diaphragm.

136  The Industry of Breath and Alignment

*Figure 5.56* A person engages their weight with the driving wheel of a car to facilitate acoustic coupling.

### Ballet Bar Experiment

1) As if you are standing up in front of a ballet bar, recreate the position that a driver of a racecar adopts. You are basically sitting in the air, legs bent at 90°, with your arms lengthened but not rigid.
2) Holding onto the ballet bar and avoiding pulling the bar with effort, simply engage your own weight with the bar as if you were gently drawing it towards you at the same time as you produce your Natural Pitch sound.

*Figure 5.57* A person resisting a ballet bar for acoustic coupling.

## Foo Dog Experiment

This experiment helps you to align the column of air and the column of sound with maximum lower abdominal pelvic floor support and diaphragm. The Foo Dog image is a paramount tool to help you to attain optimal abdominal and Intercostal Breathing, in Conditioned Breathing and voice production. Visualizing the Foo Dog body position will assist you in exploring this experiment.

*Figure 5.58* A traditional Chinese sculpture of a Foo Dog representing the depth of abdominal breathing.

### *Preparation*

- Start standing up in first ballet position.
- Do a deep grand plié, with your heels ending up naturally off the floor.
- Place the palms of your hands on the floor approximately 1.5 feet away from your toes. Your elbows should be soft, not locked in.
- Both your thumbs should be in contact as if creating the bottom edge of a tablet while the rest of your fingers spread out broadly as if mimicking a starfish.

### Process and Stages

Inhale:

1) Feel most of your body weight on your pinkies as you allow the air to come into you as with Inner Tube/Buddha Belly. The spine should be simply relaxed, concaved, with the weight of the head hanging loose, heavy and with no tension. Your weight is fully in your pinkies and the pelvic floor.
2) Inhale through your nose on six counts. For the first three counts direct your attention to the abdomen. For the last three think of your Gills and your scapulae as if you had "Hey Arnold's" head set right inside in the upper area of your torso just below the base of your neck.

### Imagery

- A Foo Dog sculpture.
- Hey Arnold's football-shaped head.
- A barrel of the most precious cognac.

*Figure 5.59* Images representing Foo Dog abdominal inhaling.

Exhale:

3) On the exhale, your weight will be slowly and gently transferred to your big toes and to the palms of your hands.

4) Over a nine count transfer your weight very slowly from your pinkies onto your big toes. Feel the weight also coming onto your hands and slightly soft arms. Do this unfolding of your spine in synchronicity with your breath.
5) As your body weight is slowly being transferred forward to your big toes, arms and hands make sure that each vertebra in your spine is being hoisted and lengthened one by one progressively from your sacrum–lumbar–thoracic–cervical as if having "pneumatic air bubbles" in between each one of them, until you find your spine fully organized at a 45°angle by the end of the nine counts.
6) Exhale twice on tempered breath with "S," followed by two more on "NG," and ending up with two on "NGA."
7) When you finish the sequence, sit up on the floor, shake your ankles and allow yourself to sigh as naturally as it suits you from the effort of the experiment.

*Imagery*

- A Foo Dog sculpture.
- The telescopic motion of a fire truck ladder as it gets extended progressively, foot by foot, on a 45° angle against the façade of a building.
- A 45° rocket-launching ramp.
- A fiddle fern uncoiling in slow motion.

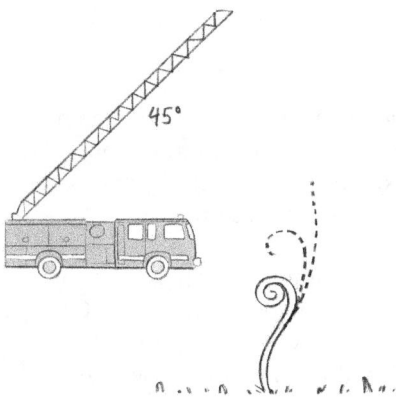

*Figure 5.60* Images representing Foo Dog exhaling spine position.

### Cornerstones

- Notice how blatantly your pelvic floor assists your sound production and how your windpipe opens your sound as it unfolds progressively.
- There is no deeper abdominal breathing possible as this experiment allows you to create the maximum amount of space in your body for the diaphragm to contract downwards.
- Make sure that your cervical belt is fully aligned and lengthened with the rest of your spine to avoid the tendency of "guillotine/flamingo" neck, which will strongly alter the optimal quality of sound you want to produce.

*Figure 5.61* Avoid flamingo neck always.

- Your gaze should be as if you were watching a spike mark on the floor 6–7 feet away ahead from you.
- When you exhale, use the full length of your breath until your "amber light" tells you to stop.

\* If for some reason this experiment is hard for you to do, there are modifications to employ to fit your needs. Often, we can translate placing your sitz bones on the edge of a chair with your hands on your knees and your arms unlocked with soft elbows.

## Notes

1. Appoggio is a form of breath support coming from the Italian word 'appoggiare' meaning 'to lean on' or 'to support'.
2. Notice I did not say "articulation," which is an artificial way to deliver sounds. There is a major difference between saying, "*articulate* the word, *articulate* the phrase" and "*pronounce* the word, *pronounce* the phrase."
3. With your right hand, create the shape of the capital letter "L." Your thumb should rest on your right collarbone while your index finger should lightly touch the middle of your chin, which is in the "Shower Mouth" position. The index and middle finger of your left hand should rest on your Adam's apple so that you register the high–middle–low movements of your larynx.
4. Edward T Hall, *The Hidden Dimension*.
5. The voiced is made by the vibration of vocal cords, like a "Z" sound, while the unvoiced or voiceless sound is the opposite, a sound with no laryngeal vibration like a "S." While making these sounds, place your finger on your Adam's apple to better perceive the difference.
6. *Fortissimo:* very loudly.
7. Zeami Motokiyo (c.1363–1443), son of Kan'ami, were the creators of what we know today as classic traditional Japanese Noh theater.

Chapter 6

# The Foundational Pillars
## The Body Sources

### From Chaos to Order: The Body Source

The task of the performer is to be able to deliver expressive material for the stage consistently and on command. Early on as a voice researcher and performer, this became a real challenge in my training with the Roy Hart Theatre. Sometimes, in my one-on-one voice lessons, it would take an entire hour to attain a particular sound. Finding my way back to it in the next session could take just as long. Once I was in the rehearsal, the luxury to explore was gone and I felt I had to deliver on cue. To solve this obstacle, I developed and established a finite matrix of sounds out of the infinite possibilities available to the human voice. This, plus discovering the concept of the **Source Point**[1] in my acupuncture studies, is how the notion of the **Body Source** came to my rescue.

The Body Source, in conjunction with Fiction and News, constitutes the **three pillars** of the Barrantes Voice System. The "Body Source," as its name indicates, is the geographic location in the body where a specific sound can be found and produced. This specific location or physical gesture in the body of the performer acts as a direct line to unlock a specific Vocal Texture.

The voice is invisible, and therefore the *memory of how it feels* – its phenomenology – is very relevant in our **métier** as performers. Practically speaking, the idea of "how something feels" is the only reliable method for its apprehension. The Body Source acts like the physical and kinesthetic support that organizes and makes tangible the psychosomatic[2] process informing one's voice. The Body Source is a free ticket for encountering possibility: a granted passport to enter the vacant imaginative and emotional chambers

DOI: 10.4324/9781003376842-7

*Figure 6.1* Draw from the Body Source to reach a specific sound.

of our singular imaginations. It acts as the connective tissue between the body, the breath, the voice, and the imagination of the performer.

The Body Source contributes to the formation of "muscle memory." Repetition is necessary to understand where the sound, or Vocal Texture, resides in the body. Both hemispheres of our brain must process and include this new information, and this is only relevant once the body has repeated this action many times.

Within each Vocal Texture is a low, middle, and high range. Finding the middle pitches within the Vocal Texture's range optimizes both your effort and labor. The ideal performer will have a Body Source for each Vocal Texture in their voice repertoire. One can think of the ensemble of Body Sources as a reliable bank of sounds to draw upon for various needs in the profession (character work, animation, voice acting, sounds in *extremis*, etc.).

The Body Source demystifies the notion of inducing an internal emotional state to perform it. Instead, accessing a specific sound or Vocal Texture through the Body Source "places" you right away into a state of vocal transformation. In other words, the Body

Source acts like a "muscle" of psychosomatic transformation and as a scaffold to support the work you are going to build for your solo or your scene. This state, plus the addition of Fiction and News, allows the performer to navigate emotional states rendering them "visible."

Remember: The Body Source offers a path to the performer to make tangible the emotional quality of a given sound through a repeatable, physical action. The Body Source mission is to attain and unlock a specific sound regardless of the performer's state of being, almost like a "password" connecting the performer directly, without any detours, to a given quality of sound. The Body Source is an amalgam, a specific "geographical" location in your body where there is a unique, unquestionable, and synergetic connection between the gesture, the breath, the sounds, and the images evoked by the Body Source.

Expressed as an equation:

*Body Source = Body + Breath + Voice + Image*

### The Voice Textures and their Body Sources

In terms of pitch, Water is the lowest Voice Texture and Air is the highest Voice Texture and they expand over five octaves in the human voice. Both Water and Air are also the most complex and advanced of the Voice Textures and that is why they are the very last Voice Textures we learn.

Even though in the training you might progress in a different manner, for the purpose of this book we will engage with the Five Voice Textures in the following order:

*Earth, Wood, Metal, Air, Water*

### Earth

If your Natural Pitch is "located" at your navel, Earth sounds encompass pitches around your Natural Pitch. You can envision the voice texture of Earth sounds as if they are coming from your pelvis. The upper tones of Earth will include all five to seven consecutive half-steps "above" your navel reaching towards your sternum. The lower tones of Earth will be the reverse. As you go down from your Natural Pitch, they will include the five to seven half-steps towards your pubis.

The Earth texture will allow you to feel grounded and dropped into your body; empowered in your own unambiguous assurance, certitude, truth, and clarity. This will evoke gravitas, calmness, weight, embodiment, gravidness, ease, and peace. Use the key image of a Buddha belly as a jumping off point to give you a sense of where Earth emanates from in your body, yet ultimately allow your imagination to take you to the images that work for you.

*Figure 6.2* Locations of Earth sounds.

## Process and Stages

1) Have your spine fully lengthened and aligned. Your body should be tonic with Fiction and your "Dantien" present and energized. Start in Neutral Position, feet parallel together. Knees slightly soft. Avoid thinking of inhaling, and instead allow the air to come into you. Have News and Fiction and only then . . .
2) Jump one foot up in the air and land *silently and softly* with your feet apart in second position. Knees slightly bent and arms reaching out like the arms of a clock at an inverted 10:10. Imagine your pelvic floor resting on a horse's back (like in Chi Kung). See image of an inverted 10:10 position.

146  The Foundational Pillars: The Body Sources

3) As you land, release simultaneously your Natural Pitch on: "NGA" with Shower Mouth and Tongue #3 at 40%.
4) Explore **Image Words** from your text.

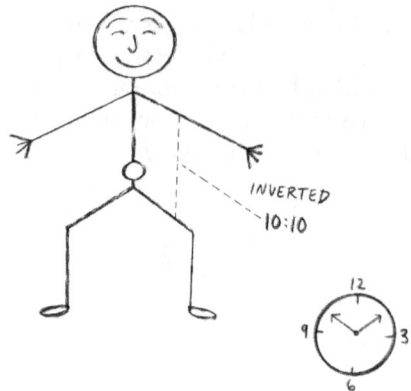

*Figure 6.3* The inverted 10:10 arm position for Earth.

To get out of the Body Source:

5) Bend your torso to the left side, allowing the right arm to become perpendicular to the ceiling. Allow your right leg to join your left leg (one foot apart) while simultaneously your right arm and torso come down toward your knees ending in a concave position in relation to the floor in one fluid sweeping motion.
6) Unwind and slowly build up your spine until you finish in the same Neutral Position as you started.

### *Imagery*

- The globe of the Earth hovering in the center of your pelvis.
- Your pelvis is heavy, gravid, as if it is ballast or "made" of heavy dark clay.
- A pregnant belly, a Buddha belly, a beer belly.
- Botero paintings or the Venus of Willendorf.

## Voice Cooling Off

- Do a series of comfortable runs gliding down on "M," "N," "NG," and "NGA."
- Do the same using trills.
- Revert to your Natural Pitch and hum on it.
- Hydrate yourself.

## Cornerstones

- *Natural Pitch and News.*
- *"Land softly and silently"* – This means to thoroughly avoid the natural clunking sound your feet will make as you land on the floor. This idea, as banal as it may sound, is critical to properly support the sound.
- *"Absorb the shock on landing"* – Land silently on your feet. You should have the same quality of excellence as the shock absorbers of any of those top-of-the-line luxury cars (think Rolls Royce, BMW, Maserati, etc.).
- *"Fiction in the body"* – If you avoid that natural clunking sound, your body has Fiction. Having Fiction with this action means that your sound and body have the full support of both your pelvic floor as well as your diaphragm at 40% on Tongue #3.
- *"Dantien"* – Remember from our exploration of the abdomen in Chapter 4 that your Dantien connects you to your center of gravity, giving you energy, and poised stability.

## Listening References

- Johnny Cash: *"Hurt," "Ring of Fire."*
- Leonard Cohen: *"Suzanne."*
- Serge Gainsbourg: *"Melody"* from *"Histoire de Melodie Nelson."*
- Alberta Hunter: *"My Handy Man," "Sweet Georgia Brown."*
- Odetta: *"I Know Where I Am Going."*
- Chavela Vargas: *"La Llorona," "Macorina."*
- Barry White: *"Can't Get Enough of Your Love, Babe."*

## Broken Earth

Envision this sound as the result of a sudden, short, intense, and release. It is the result of letting your Natural Pitch and the diaphragm go all at once and without any "brakes" stopping it. Therefore, I describe this texture as "broken." The ventricular bands of your larynx participate strongly in the production of this sound and requires you to have News.

Broken Earth can be a very gratifying sound. Think of it as a joyous and wonderfully transgressive texture, as if it is at the ancestral threshold between being animal and human. It should be effortless and much like a "vomit of sound" that spills out of you rather than being forced. Your body should be hypotonic, playful, relaxed, and using positive emotions. Avoid working with "negative" emotions. The reason being (since you may do this on your own) is that I cannot guarantee you will be producing this sound correctly without any psychosomatic risks involved.

Give yourself plenty of time to deal with, dig, and dive into this sound using positive emotions and News, so that your technique gets well established. The classroom and rehearsal space are the ideal environments to approach this Voice Texture.

### *Process and Stages*

There are three different ways to experience the Body Source of Broken Earth:

 I. Release from a standing-up position.
 II. Release from medium level.
 III. Release at floor level.

Find which one works best for you.

### *I. Broken Earth Release from Standing-Up Position*

We will conduct this Body Source on a four count, and with a slightly unique breathing pattern of *inhale–inhale–exhale–exhale* (the amount of air/breath needed to support this energized sound requires full inhalation and exhalation, hence the double inhales and exhales each time).

## The Foundational Pillars: The Body Sources 149

Before you start the following four steps take one last inhale on Relative Position. By the end of the exhale, find yourself "eclipsed" and ready to launch with your arms out on an inverted 10:10.

1) On Count 1 as you inhale, maintain your Relative Position with soft knees so your body can bounce and benefit from gravity's pull on your own body weight. Arms out at an inverted 10:10. [Avoid thinking of inhaling. Allow your breath to cascade into you instead. Have News and Fiction and only then...] Allow the air of Count 1 to come into you, your legs still in demi-plié. Cross your arms up and inwardly (towards and in front your face) 3/4 of a circle around, until they end perpendicular to the ceiling, pointing to the sky (your wrists will cross one another during the arms' journey until they end up perpendicular to the ceiling, completing three quarters of the circle around).
2) On Count 2 you inhale again (like "topping off" a gas tank) as you demi-plié/bounce the knees again and change the direction of your arms, letting them go down forward, swinging them up, and finishing again perpendicular to the ceiling.
3) On Count 3, as you exhale, your torso from waist up does a ballistic projection forward. However, from the waist down, your legs are flexed and your feet in parallel position are going to remain firm holding your weight. The arms are going to go down simultaneously with the ballistic projection of your torso. From being above your head they will end up behind and beside your torso, which is now nearer the floor.

In fact, your torso is going to be concave in relation to the floor like the image of a skier slaloming down a mountain slope. This ballistic projection should have a passive feeling of gravidness.

Make sure you have Shower Mouth, with a relaxed jaw at less than the regular, supported sound of 40%, i.e., aiming for 30%. Image is paramount at this moment. During the exhale on this count, you allow your Natural Pitch sound (which is Earth) to "break" by saying one of the following in a BROKEN EARTH voice: *grunt, brat, frat,* brooo, frooog, crooog, grooow, *whaaasup, cookies.*[3]

The tongue in fact is on a Tongue Position #2.3 or #2.5, however once you experience the sound and are going to use it on stage, I recommend you stay on Tongue Position #3 so that there will not be a question of ever hurting yourself with this texture.

4) On this final count as you exhale you simply bounce and indulge where you arrived on the previous count. Release your body down as you exhale a second time in this position, repeating the word you just said in Step 3. Shower Mouth and image are paramount for you to experience this texture. At the tail end of your bounce, your arms are going to do a sweeping motion ending up forwards at their starting position. On the *and*/half-beat following this fourth count, hoist your body up again and start the cycle all over again.

5) Explore Image Words from your text on the third and fourth count.

### *Imagery*

- Anything that encourages images of release and abandonment.
- Cookie Monster.
- Large dog barking.
- Soft growling, groaning.

### *Cooling Off*

- Do a series of comfortable runs gliding down on "M," "N," "NG," and "NGA."
- Revert to your Natural Pitch and hum with it.
- Do the same using trills.
- Hydrate yourself.

### *Cornerstones*

- Remember it is a release with Shower Mouth and Tongue #3 at 30%.
- Image is paramount for you to experience this Voice Texture.
- Fiction and News.
- Four counts: Inhale–Inhale–Exhale–Exhale.

## II. Broken Earth Release from Medium Level

This approach is done with two people. One person is "monitor," the other is "doer."

### THE MONITOR ROLE

1) The Monitor is going to start in Relative Position, extending both arms fully and comfortably, reaching for and holding their hands gently on the iliac crest (hip bone) of the Doer, much like the arms of a Formula One driver.
2) Soft elbows, soft knees, and heels fully on the floor. The Monitor is going to make sure that the Doer is going to fully abandon their weight to the Monitor. For this, the Monitor is going to gently sway the pelvis in all four directions until the Doer has given up their weight. The feeling should be as if a 200-pound plastic garbage bag was full of water, and we tried to gently sway it. Naturally so, the volume of water moves in one piece and wobbles, full of gravity. That is what we want to experience between Monitor and Doer.

### THE DOER ROLE

3) The Doer bends the torso forwards, parallel to the floor, and arms hanging loose or folded. Heels planted on the floor. They should feel much like a swimmer prior to diving in the water. The Doer should trust the Monitor holding their hips and weight. Give yourselves plenty of time to feel this association and complicity between you both.
4) Once this connection between Monitor and Doer is established, the Monitor is going to say to the Doer, "I let go." At that moment, the Monitor releases the hips of the Doer and allows the Doer to fall to the ground, "catching" themselves with their hands (without letting the knees touch the ground), ending in a hovered all-fours position. The Doer at that very moment of "landing" should release one of the following words: "brooo, frooog, gruuunt, braaat, fraaat, moii, whassup, Cookies" or use Image Words from your text.

152   The Foundational Pillars: The Body Sources

VARIATION #1 WITHOUT THE ASSISTANCE OF THE MONITOR:

On all fours, implement three to four times the landing of the element described above: "I let go." Absorb the shock of the landing with soft elbows, head and neck relaxed. As you land choose between the following words: "brooo, frooog, gruuunt, braaat, fraaat, whassup, Cookies." You may also try this in the same way but using your body as a worm moving forward on the floor as in a break dance.

### *Imagery*

- Anything that encourages images of release and abandonment.
- Cookie Monster.
- Large dog barking.
- Soft growling, groaning.

### *Cooling Off*

- Do a series of comfortable runs gliding down on "M," "N," "NG," and "NGA."
- Do the same using trills.

### *Cornerstones*

- This is a release, a fall. Similar to how the weight of the body is "thrown" into the water when someone does a cannon ball at the pool. No effort being employed. Simply pure body weight. No big risk involved.
- Avoid the splattering sound of the hands when landing. Your hands and arms should totally act as "high-end shock absorbers" and land in a starfish shape. Erase **biography**. The simultaneity of the sound with the landing is *crucial*.
- The position you arrive at landing should be exactly as if you were "on all fours," except the knees are one to two inches off the floor not allowing them to touch the ground. Observe perfect 90° between all different joints: feet with legs, legs with knees, thighs with pelvis, pelvis with torso, shoulders with arms.
- The head and the neck must stay relaxed.

## III. Broken Earth Release on Floor Level

I very rarely encourage a Body Source based on a psychosomatic emotional state of being because of its potential unreliability; however, this Body Source tends to work for many people who find the coordination of Method 1 challenging and do not have a partner to use for Method 2, so here we go:

1) Simply evoke and explore the image of being a slightly happy and silly tipsy person. This is before that state when you hardly realized you are totally "plastered."
2) You are lying on your back on the floor and can barely sit up, you giggle, you indulge in the feeling of being so heavy, tired, energy-less yet joyous. You can hardly stand due to how heavy your whole body feels. You barely can move one hand up, let alone the whole arm. You abandon your weight and roll side to side on the floor. Utter repeatedly, with enjoyment, the expression: "Oh myyy Gooooood! I can't believe thiiiiis! OMG!! How am I going to get uuuup?"
3) You laugh again, surrender to your lack of muscular tonus, and let us hear the broken sound that accompanies such a state of being. Sway from your right to left, side-to-side, heavy, and stuporous . . .
4) Explore Image Words from your text.

### Imagery

- Feeling extremely heavy in your body.
- A very fast sudden release of a Venetian blind rolled up like in a cartoon.
- Joyous, relaxed, and exhausted sound after climbing five flights of stairs with large grocery shopping bags.

### Cooling Off

- Do a series of comfortable runs gliding down on "M," "N," "NG," and "NGA."
- Do the same using trills.

### Cornerstones

- Rock gently and drunkenly your body sitting up on the floor side to side, much like a boat rocking gently in the marina.
- Being happily and kindly plastered sitting on the floor.

### Listening References

- Cookie Monster from *Sesame Street*.
- *"The Unstoppable Tennis Grunt."*
- Tom Waits: *"Lucky Day."*

### Strong Wood

Envision Wood sounds as coming from your torso. Pitch-wise, this Voice Texture relates to the medium register of your natural voice.

I describe it as "strong" because the sound quality relates to the medium–strong intensity or volume in which the sound is being produced. In musical terminology this "strong" quality is the equivalent of "mezzo forte" or medium-loud. It should not be confused with a natural tendency to belt. That will fall more into the category of loud, very loud, or very strong quality of sound.

Like with any other sound Body Source, you want to produce the sound in the most comfortable, beneficial, and aligned manner possible. Connecting your form (Body Source) to imagery and intuitive approach is crucial to ease the production of the sound. As usual make sure that you erase your biographical elements by precisely executing this Body Source.

### Process and Stages

The **pitch** of Wood is, on average, between the fifth and the octave above your Natural Pitch.

Start the experiment exploring three different pitches: one high, one middle, and one low. Do not alter the intensity of sound. Maintain Shower Mouth at 40% on Tongue #3.

After doing so a couple of times, you should be able to perceive in your voice and your body where is the most ideal, comfortable tone for you to release a Strong Wood sound. You want an effortless mid-range pitch that is well centered, aligned, solid and energetic.

Remember: You should never belt it or shout it (60%–80%) unless you want to do so to get it out of your system, to notice how strained it feels, or to consciously understand what to avoid doing in your practice.

**Lower Strong Wood Tones** will include on average four consecutive half-tones starting a fifth above one's Natural Pitch.

Imagine these tones coming from the low part of your torso, something like two to three inches above your navel and the floating ribs.

**Middle Strong Wood Tones**, which are the ones you primarily want to work with, will include, on average, four consecutive half-tones starting from where you left off with the low Strong Wood sounds.

Imagine this middle comfortable register of Strong Wood tones resides around six inches above your navel (the same height where the floating ribs are in your torso) and ends right at the bottom tip of your sternum, the xiphoid process.

**Upper Strong Wood Tones** will include, on average, four consecutive half-tones starting where the Middle pitch left off.

Imagine this range as residing at the bottom tip of the sternum and ending at the top tip of your sternum, between your clavicles, the manubrium.

This Body Source uses the image of throwing an imaginary ripe fruit or small water balloon.

1) Start in your Relative Position, feet parallel. If you are right-handed, you will place the left leg slightly forward, comfortably bent. Your left kneecap is aligned above and between your big toe and your pinky, while the right leg is simply lengthened but not stiff. Use your natural gate, distributing your weight evenly between your front and back legs. Feel solid, like a tree. These steps will strengthen your throwing.

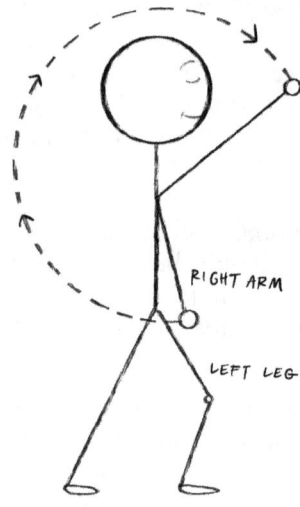

STRONG WOOD

*Figure 6.4* Strong Wood position with arm placement.

Make sure your spine is lengthened and aligned with your pelvis. Your torso should be exactly in the middle, between the front leg and the back leg, to give you a steady, firm, and poised torso. Avoid tension and make sure that you feel the ensemble of your feet engaged both to your body (via the Dantien) and to the ground. You will initiate the throw with your arm opposite to the leg in front. Both iliac crests of your pelvis should be aligned on the same frontal plane. Avoid *biographical* elements in your throw; this will help align your voice.

The throw you are about to do should be very clean, impersonal, un-psychological and devoid of *biography*; much like a 100-meter sprinter Olympic athlete awaiting the signal to start running. No force is needed, simply allow gravity to do the work for you. You are now well planted, centered, and gravid, just the same way in which a chimney is built over a hearth. Avoid any curves, tilting forward, or allowing *biographical* idiosyncrasies.

2) You are now ready to throw with your right arm (if you are right-handed) a soft, ripe, large tomato, or a papaya, against a

wall opposite you so that you will make it splatter with great gusto and a sense of release.

Your right arm and fist, gently cupping the invisible fruit, is hanging by your thigh. Inhale. Your arm is going to do a 180° circle ending up above your head.

Only your arm will do the throwing, without intervention of the shoulders, hips, or torso participating in the action. Your spine is fully lengthened; your core is tonic and aligned. Your Dantien is energized. Avoid thinking of inhaling, and instead allow the air to come into you. Have News and Fiction and only then...

Your throw should have vigorous energy. I imagine the sound of the tomato against the wall: "schlaaack!" Now you release the soft ripe fruit, in that very split second as you exhale (this synchronicity is very important), you allow the sound "NGA" on Shower Mouth at 40% and Tongue #3 to be released. Sustain it for six to seven seconds. Use Image Words from your text.

3) After those six to seven seconds, when the "amber light" of your sound sends the message to your brain that you need a new breath, only at that moment do you stop the sound. Let your torso and right arm release down to the floor, simultaneously bringing the right leg next to your front left.

Inhale and unwind your spine up until you attain the original Relative Position you started with.

## *Imagery*

Throw against a wall across from yourself:

- Very soft ripe tomato, persimmon, papaya, chirimoya.
- Small hand-sized water balloon.
- Large soft carrot cake.
- Large egg.

## *Cooling Off*

- Do a series of comfortable runs gliding down on "M," "N," "NG," and "NGA."

- Do the same using trills.
- Revert to your Natural Pitch and hum with it.
- Hydrate yourself.

### Cornerstones

- Fiction and News.
- Both iliac crests aligned on the same plane.
- Medium comfortable pitch.
- Shower Mouth, Tongue #3 at 40%.
- Synchronicity between the throwing and the sound is paramount.
- Get into and go out of the Body Source properly.
- Only the arm accomplishes the throwing.
- Give News to the throw.

### Listening References

- Coldplay: *"Viva La Vida."*
- Aretha Franklin: *"Natural Woman."*
- John Lennon: *"Mother," "Stand by Me."*
- Odetta: *"Motherless Child."*
- Astor Piazzolla / Amelita Baltar: *"Balada para un loco."*
- Queen: *"Bohemian Rhapsody," "Save Me."*
- Amy Winehouse: *"Rehab."*

## Soft Wood

The Soft Wood Body Source is a very logical, simple, straightforward consequence of Strong Wood. All that you must do is to allow less intensity on the note you started with Strong Wood. Think of it as a "melting" of the Strong Wood sound.

Fundamentally you are going to repeat steps 1 and 2 as described in Strong Wood Body Source and sustain the sound for 4 to 6 seconds.

### Process and Stages

1) Begin with Strong Wood. Arrive at the point where you are sustaining Strong Wood for 4–6 seconds. Then, allow your sound

to become softer and the transition to Soft Wood occurs. For the next 4–6 seconds, after you start it at 40%, allow the sound to become half of the original intensity, finishing it at 20%. Maintain your Shower Mouth as you do this. Allow your right wrist and arm to "melt" to illustrate the softening of the sound. Use Image Words from your text.

2) After those 8–12 seconds, when the "amber light of your sound" comes on, stop the Soft Wood sound, letting your torso and right arm release down towards the floor. Simultaneously bring the right leg next to your front left, inhale and unwind your spine up until you return to the original Relative Position you began with.

### *Imagery*

- Private or personal level of intensity of sound.
- Soft, gentle vocal energy like the branch of a willow.
- Crooning mood.

### *Cooling Off*

- Revert to your Natural Pitch and hum with it.
- Hydrate yourself.

### *Cornerstones*

- No sense of projection.
- Fiction and News.
- Create your own soft, gentle, "melted" Body Source.

### *Listening References*

- Billie Holiday: "Strange Fruit."
- Chet Baker: "My Funny Valentine."
- John Lee Hooker: "The Waterfront."
- Nina Simone: "Just Say I Love Him," "Who Knows Where the Time Goes."
- Liz Wright: "A Taste of Honey."
- Suzanne Vega: "Tom's Diner" and "Luka."
- Navajo Healing Song, Lakota Peyote Healing Song.

## Broken Wood

The Broken Wood Voice Texture is the organic, natural next step regarding your breath after exploring Soft Wood. In Broken Wood, you are running out of breath until the sound becomes like the sound of sizzling popcorn.

This Voice Texture is unlike any of the others, in that I suggest you go through the "amber light" of your sound/breath to experience this texture. The result, due to the hypotonicity of your voice as you run out of breath, is not unlike that of "**glottal fry**." Your vocal folds are closing tightly together, and their edges produce free "bubbly" sounds.

These sounds are reminiscent of sizzling popcorn, an idle chainsaw, an old door's hinged creaking, the sound of wooden planks on a deck, or dry pipes in a Mediterranean summerhouse. It is a sound that children often make to space out from their environment.

It is a hypnotic, mesmerizing sound that perfectly blends with hyper-realistic, fantastical, animated types of creatures.

This is schematically speaking the sound progression of finding this Voice Texture:

*Strong Wood ---- > Soft Wood ---- > Broken Wood*

### Process and Stages

1) You are going to repeat the steps of Strong Wood into Soft Wood picking up when the "amber light" of your sound/breath comes on. Simply continue the sound, making sure that you try to maintain the pitch of the original Strong Wood sound, which then became Soft Wood, and now is ready to transform into a Broken Wood sound.

    The break of the sound happens because you are running out of breath, so there is no other possibility for the sound to do anything else but to break.

    Go through that mysterious playful threshold and give into the sound as it breaks, so that you create your own strange, weird, almost contorted Body Source for it. Illustrate with your body the inner image you are giving voice to, allowing

yourself to physicalize the inner landscape this sound creates. Trust your intuitive intelligence. Do not think, just follow your instincts, and let your body create a personalized Body Source.
2) Alternate several times between your Relative Position and your own Broken Wood Body Source so that you create body memory. Once you understand this Body Source, go from Relative into the Broken Wood Body Source, and begin to play with text, **paralinguistics**, and/or song. Use Image Words from text.

### Imagery

- Use private or personal level of intensity of sound only.
- Envision hyper-realistic, fantastical cartoon-like creatures, i.e., the Hobbit.
- A wooden object cracking or crackling, a plank, a wooden board, a door, a boat rocking slowly on the harbor, an idle chainsaw, popcorn sizzling . . .

### Cooling Off

- Do a series of comfortable runs gliding down on "M," "N," "NG," and "NGA."
- Do the same using trills.
- Revert to your Natural Pitch and hum with it.
- Hydrate yourself.

### Cornerstones

- Fiction and News.
- As your Soft Wood sound runs out of breath, make sure you try to maintain the same pitch as the sound begins to break – avoid the temptation to do go down into glottal fry; keep in mind the pitch should still be in your mid-Wood range.

### Listening References

- I recommend you look up the zombie-esque monsters from "The Last of Us" and witness the sounds they create.

## Epic Hollow Wood

Envision the porous sound that a hollow redwood or sequoia tree could possibly make. Hollow Wood sounds belong to your torso. This beautiful sound has the following attributes: warmth, nurturing, beauty, velvet-like, softness, fruity, and hollowness.

I always preface this Body Source by listening to the recording of Cecilia Bartoli singing "Sposa" from *Vivaldi's Bajazet*.

### Process and Stages

Use eight counts when doing this Body Source. You are going to be singing the word "Sposa," singing the first four counts with the syllable "SPO-O-O-O" and the last four counts singing the syllable "SA-A-A-A." Remember to have your spine lengthened and use Shower Mouth with Tongue #3 at 40%. Recommended interval: $B^b4$–E4. Avoid thinking of inhaling, and instead allow the air to come into you. Have News and Fiction and only then . . . (on $B^b4$):

First four counts of this Body Source singing: "SPO-O-O-O" on $B^b4$:

1) **Count 1** on "SPO." Stand up in the first position as you sing the first count. Spine lengthened all the way like the Eiffel Tower.
2) **Count 2** on "O." Shift your weight fully to the left side and tilt your lengthened body as if to recreate the Tower of Pisa image.
3) **Counts 3 and 4** on "O-O." Now is the time, during these two counts, to bend your left leg while the two following actions take place simultaneously:

   a. Your right toes, barely any weight on them, are going to slide to reach the furthest point on your right side. Please make sure you do not adjust the weight of your body as you do this action.
   b. Your arms open during these two counts 45° towards an inverted 10:10 position, to balance the simultaneous motion of your right leg and toes.

Last four counts of this Body Source singing: "SA-A-A-A" on E4:

4) **Counts 5 and 6** on "SA:" Now is the time to slide the right foot further to the right side until you find yourself in a perfect demi-plié second position, with your weight evenly distributed on both legs, as if sitting on a horse's back.
During these two counts you begin to sing "SA" – hold for all four last counts.
5) **Counts 7 and 8** on "A-A-A:" You now have these last two counts to make sure that you end up with your weight absolutely centered in second plié position, as if sitting on a horse, with your arms at an inverted 10:10, as if you were embracing a large redwood or sequoia hollow tree.

Make sure you maintain Tongue #3. The quality of the sound should remain the same as you sing both syllables. The tendency is to sing the first syllable, "SPO," on Tongue #3 at 40% but to let it go into a Tongue #2.5 as you sing the second syllable "SA." Be very cautious and meticulous observing this.

To get out of the Body Source:

6) Bend your torso to the left side, allowing the right arm to become perpendicular to the ceiling. Allow your right leg to join, one foot apart, your left leg while simultaneously your right arm and torso come down toward your knees, ending in a concave position in relation to the floor. Slowly unwind your spine until you finish in the same Relative Position as you started.

### *Imagery*

- "Wedge" yourself between the bark and the body of a redwood or sequoia tree.
- Hug a redwood tree with the most possible contact of your body on its surface.
- A large sequoia hollow tree.

### *Cornerstones*

- Fiction and News.
- Shower Mouth and Tongue #3 at 40%.
- Sound attributes: warmth, nurturing, beauty, velvety texture, softness, fruity quality.

- The more meticulous and precise you are executing the Body Source, the better chance you may attain this sound.

**Cooling Off**

- Do a series of comfortable runs gliding down on "M," "N," "NG," and "NGA."
- Do the same using trills.
- Revert to your Natural Pitch and hum with it.
- Hydrate yourself.

**Listening References**

- Kathleen Ferrier: *"When I Am Laid in Earth"* from Purcell's *"Dido and Aeneas."*
- Marian Anderson: *"Der Döppelganger"* and *"Ave Maria"* by Schubert.
- Cecilia Bartoli: *"Sposa son Disprezzata"* from Vivaldi's *"Bajazet."*
- Jakub Józef Orliński: *"Vedro con Mio Diletto"* from Vivaldi's *"Il Giustino."*

**Lyric Hollow Wood**

In class, I always introduce this texture by listening to the marvelous interpretation of Handel's "Ombra Mai Fu" by Kathleen Ferrier. This voice texture is tentative, delicate, tender, and intimate. It evokes solemn wonder, profound devotion, and longing. Men might have a harder time allowing the texture to settle in, but when they experience Lyric Hollow Wood, it causes deep awe. It is very productive regarding emotional research for a scene or to simply expand, at large, your emotional range.

**Process and Stages**

1) This texture works best when you create your own individualized Body Source. Be very simple, restrained, committed. Approach it as if you were exhaling, unfolding, soaring, expanding very slowly. This Body Source is about your own inner world.

2) Avoid thinking of inhaling. Instead allow the air to come into you. Have News and Fiction and only then...start around G#4 on a *pianissimo* intensity. Start singing "Ombra Mai Fu" on Tongue #2.
3) As you continue to sing the aria, allow Tongue #3 to come in but without force, always extremely soft and delicate, privileging that feeling of longing that Ferrier conveys on her opening sound.

### Imagery

- Delight, abundance, boundlessness, ethereal, longing, devotion, cherishing.
- Deeply poetic, lyrical, full of longing and kindness.

### Cornerstones

- Fiction and News.
- Sound attributes of warmth, nurturing, velvety texture, softness, fruity quality.
- Shower Mouth and Tongue #2 becomes Tongue #3 at 20%.

### Cooling Off

- Do a series of comfortable runs gliding down on "M," "N," "NG," and "NGA."
- Do the same using trills; revert to your Natural Pitch and hum with it.
- Hydrate yourself.

### Listening References

- Kathleen Ferrier: *"Ombra Mai Fu."*
- Coloratura: *"Una Voce Poco Fa."*

## Metal

Envision the Metal Voice Texture as residing in the head, with the following sound attributes: piercing, pinging, bright, forward.

This is a very rich yet taxing Voice Texture. The vocal identities expressed in Metal are fundamentally those belonging to farce, caricature, and hyper-real worlds such as cartoons, animation characters, video games, etc. Keep in mind that Metal at 100% falls into the realm of parody, extremely comedic, exaggerated, mockery, phony, burlesque, and a "put-on" voice, etc.

Since it is a rather challenging Vocal Texture, it is going to be very useful to understand a couple of concepts before we start to describe the Body Source itself. The key for us is to understand the difference between **Nasal quality** and **Nasality** *(or **Nasalization**)*. German voice teacher and opera singer Lilli Lehmann[4] would teach that a singer must possess some nasal quality to add color and expression to their voice.

> **Nasal quality** can be considered a vital part of the whole resonating system that gives brilliance and power to the voice. It is also a major component of the so-called "mask resonance." Because of its power though, it can dominate and distort the timbre of the sound and turn into *nasalization*.
>
> **Nasality** *(or **Nasalization**)* is when the soft palate becomes soft, flaccid, resting in the far back area of the tongue, obstructing the nasal passage, and making the sound "adenoidal." Another cause might be due to the root of the tongue bulging up at the back of the mouth.

On this topic, it will be to your advantage to understand the following three basic qualities:

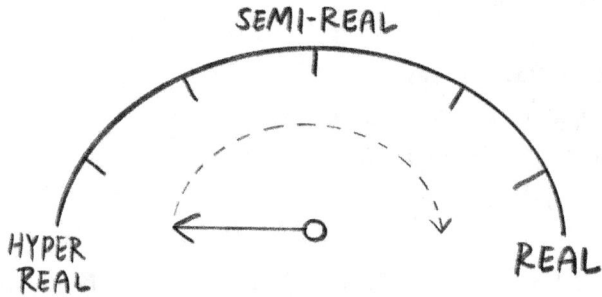

*Figure 6.5* The three levels of applying Metal.

|  1  |  2  |  3  |
|---|---|---|
| Full Hyperreal ------> | Medium Hyperreal ------> | Realistic |
| 100% Metal ------> | 60% Metal ------> | 40% Metal |

*Figure 6.6* **Percentages given to each level of Metal.**

As a performer, you want to master the whole spectrum of this Voice Texture, from caricature to earnest, sincere, natural, and realistic rendering. To attain this, begin to speak or sing at a 100% hyper-real, cartoon-like quality. After that, progressively withdraw the exaggerated brightness of the sound. Do this until the point in which the Metal sound could easily pass for a sound that still has the brightness of Metal but can be considered real, natural, and honest.

## Process and Stages

*1) Starting Position*
Stand up and align your body in your Relative Position. Let the torso hang over your feet, head around your knees' level. Soft knees. Let gravity do the work.

*2) The "N" Sound and Placement*
Gravity by itself is going to make you aware of your blood building in pressure behind your forehead and eyes. Pay attention to this specific area, your "third eye," between and slightly above your eyes.

In that position, allow a very easy, natural sound of Metal to come out. Use the phoneme "N" and sustain it. Tip of the tongue behind upper incisors. Aim always for your medium range. If the sound you produce is too high, you are going to be making a tremendous effort and the sound will be strident. If you approach it from too low a range, it will have the quality of high Wood.

Allow the sound to come to you as a result of the blood congesting behind your third eye. On average, this pitch tends to be around an octave above your Natural Pitch. You should incorporate the bright/forward sound quality and placement of Tongue #1, but without actually arching the tongue itself forward at all. Produce this "N" sound several times both in staccato and legato mode so that you create body memory.

Useful images can include a unicorn, Pinocchio, a certain feeling of constipation, electricity current, etc.

3) *Use These Syllables: "NI-NE-NA-NO-NU"*
Keep the placement of the sound from the previous step. Relax your jaw and say the following syllables in the same Metal pitch you voiced with the "N" sound: NI-NE-NA-NO-NU (French "u" helps the nasality) and do the same sustaining, as in singing, each syllable.

The next step is using Image Words like Nina, Nickel, knee, Nefertiti, Nashville, new, Newark, or any Image Words from your text.

4) *Come back to Relative Position*
Keep playing with the sounds/words from the previous step while you unroll your spine upwards, vertebrae by vertebrae. Make sure you do not lose the sound you created through the previous steps.

Remember to take rests often when practicing this sound to avoid vocal fatigue.

### *Imagery*

- The horn of a unicorn protruding between your eyes.
- Pinocchio's long nose.
- Small high-pitched insects.
- Metal thread of sound, an electric cable, electricity current.
- A certain feeling of constipation.

### *Cooling Off*

Because Metal encourages your larynx to be high, it is very important that you cool off scrupulously:

- Do a series of comfortable runs gliding down on "M," "N," "NG," and "NGA."
- Do the same using trills.
- Revert to your Natural Pitch and hum with it.
- Hydrate yourself.

## Cornerstones

- Fiction and News are imperative.
- The use of imagery is essential for being able to maintain this Voice Texture.
- Rest and relax your larynx for a short period every so often so that you do not fatigue your voice.
- Avoid resisting the outrageous, **grotesque**, and farce-like quality that this voice evokes – give into the ridiculous nature it induces.

## Listening References

- Indian Culture: Rafi & Lata Shashi Kapoor & Babita, 60s Indian Cinema.
- Chinese Culture: 同光十三 Beijing Opera.
- Spanish Culture: *"Jotas Aragonesas."*
- Native American Culture: *Poundmakers Tribute Song to Devere Tsatoke.*
- Operatic Culture: Jeff Buckley *"Dido's Lament."*

## Broken Metal

(Disclaimer: Please consult with your teacher regarding this Voice Texture if you happen to be under any **psychotropic** prescription medications).

Envision this Voice Texture residing in the head, in the same region as Metal. This is an extraordinary, rather labor-intensive, but very expressive and striking Voice Texture. This Voice Texture is composed of several sounds at once, hence the denomination of "broken."

I always introduce it by playing two of Janis Joplin's great songs: "Cry Baby" or "Summertime."

## Process and Stages

*1) Starting*

Stand up and align your body in your Relative Position. Let the torso hang over your feet, head around your knees' level. Soft knees. Let gravity do the work.

## 170 The Foundational Pillars: The Body Sources

*2) The "N" Sound and Placement*

Like the Metal Body Source, remember to let gravity make you aware of the blood building in pressure behind your forehead and eyes. Pay attention to this specific area, your "third eye," between and slightly above your eyes.

Allow in that position an easy natural sound of Metal to come out. Use the sound "N." Tip of the tongue behind upper incisors. Aim always for your medium range. Produce this "N" sound several times both in staccato and legato mode so that you create body memory.

Useful images include a unicorn, Pinocchio, metal threads, and (a very useful one!) a large, prehistoric pterodactyl bird . . .

Given the obstacles involved in the Broken Metal sound, it is very helpful to subdivide this Body Source in three phases:

*3) Phase I: "Niiiiiiiiiiiiiiiiiiiiiiii" . . .*

Sustain the Metal sound with the syllable "Niiiiiiiiiiiiiiiii . . ." Try to maintain it between 8–12 seconds at a time and repeat several times to create body memory.

Envision you are a pterodactyl bird inside its own large egg. Move and wiggle your very thin long fingers as if they were laser beams around your head, exploring where the weakest area is so you can easily crack the eggshell and emerge from it.

Uncoil your spine very slowly and just before you run out of breath, find yourself standing up.

Keep your focus on the third eye area and feel the forward placement of the sound as in Tongue #1, but without arching the tongue itself forward.

Two areas are strongly involved in this sound:

- The nasopharynx.
- Your sinuses.

Remember that this type of sound has a nondaily, extraordinary acoustic nature; therefore, it needs strong News for you to be able to produce it. Repeat this several times so you can connect with it, as well as with the images that the sound suggests to you (insects, threads of metal, cartoons, etc.).

*4) Phase II: "Niiiiiiiiiiiiiiiiiiiiii . . . A" . . .*

As you find yourself standing up in Relative Position and about to run out of breath, allow your elbows to open up to your sides. Maintain the pitch you have opening up the phoneme to ". . . AAAAAA." Maintain a relaxed Shower Mouth with a sound reminiscent of the one that accompanies Tongue #1, forward in the front of your mask. Your elbows have now become small wings breaking the eggshell. The sound is going to inevitably break because you have very little breath left. That is the goal. A Broken Metal sound.

Keep the image of opening your elbows wide to break your eggshell.

Maintain only tonic muscular approach while doing this. Never hypertonic, even though it is the natural response to running out of breath. Avoid using physical effort and resist that temptation by investing in News.

5) Phase III: "SHRYyy . . . BRYy . . . CRYyy . . . GRY . . ."

As soon as the Metal sound breaks with the vowel "AAA . . .", open your arms, reaching out like the wings of the prehistorical pterodactyl. Avoid your shoulders going up. Keep your scapular connection.

Add words like: *"SHRYyy . . . BRYy . . . CRYyy . . . GRY . . ."* These syllables have that "r" sound in them which is going to help you to maintain the break of the sound.

6) Explore the sound with paralinguistics, Image Words, and take it into text using Fiction and News to assist you sustaining the sound you are producing.

7) Cool off your voice. It is very important with this Voice Texture.

### *Imagery*

- The image of a prehistoric pterodactyl is extremely helpful.

### *Cornerstones*

- Fiction and News.
- This Voice Texture uses Tongue #1, #2 and #3.
- Use pterodactyl images as News.

### *Cooling Off*

Because Metal encourages your larynx to be high, it is very important you cool off scrupulously:

- Do a series of comfortable runs gliding down on "M," "N," "NG," and "NGA."
- Do the same using trills.
- Revert to your Natural Pitch and hum with it.
- Hydrate yourself.

### Listening References

- Janis Joplin: *"Cry Baby," "I Need a Man to Love," "Summertime."*
- I also recommend listening to your favorite Rock and extreme Metal bands.

### Air

*(Disclaimer. Please consult with your teacher regarding this particular Voice Texture if you happen to be under any psychotropic prescription/medications).*

### "Basic Air Thoughts"

With Air, there is never a specific sound destination; you can only create and provide the environment. The rest is up to Air itself to let you know where to go and take you "there" because air flows constantly. There is something highly contemplative and restorative about Air sounds. It is like going back, or maybe even forward, in time to when we played freely between dream and reality (maybe in our cradles, our tiny beds, on the carpet of our rooms, or in the middle of a galaxy . . .). The sense of time and space with Air becomes warped . . . explore.

When I start working on Air, I always refer to three different breath approaches that seem very conducive to feeling the subtleties within Air.

- **Ujjayi breath** *is a soft, whisper-like type of breath slowly tempered by the diaphragm. Some yoga schools call it "ocean breath." I associate this sound with the wind blowing in the forest or in the firmament.*
- **Sirocco** *is hot air. To produce this sound, I associate it with the vowel 'ah' as if defrosting an icy window. Imagine winds/air from the desert.*

- **Glacial** *is cold wind. To produce this sound, I associate it with the delicate, weak vowel 'oh,' as in the sound of a windy snowstorm by the Matterhorn Mountain. Feel the cold air from the North and South Poles.*

## Preparing for Air

Anchor your body in a second position on demi-plié. Spine lengthened. Pelvis grounded. Energize your Dantien. Feel your weight and engage your pelvic floor. Use Shower Mouth. Close your eyes and begin to explore the previous Sirocco and Glacial winds mentioned above. Freely sway your body on the spot to illustrate these images.

If you do this alone, record it and listen to it. Allow yourself to wander and get lost in the images with eyes closed. When working as a group, listen to the manifestation of other people's images in their breath, include them in your work, and "call and respond" to each other. Simply listen to the breath and all its different temperatures and colors.

Let your upper body flow. Feel differences in your body as you do each type of wind. Work mindfully with the vowels "O" and "A" for the different temperatures and notice what actually happens in your pharynx (feel free to monitor it).

Ask yourself the following questions:

- When is your glottal passage totally open and when does it constrict?
- How does the work connect with your low abdomen (diaphragm)?
- Which muscles are working to serve the image you are creating? How?
- When does your larynx go up and when down?

## Imagery

- Envision you are Eolo, the God of the winds in Greek mythology, sending all sorts of winds to the Earth from far away in the cosmos. You are giving the humans their four seasons.
- Vast spaces, cosmic, galactic, etc.

- Small spaces, like a crack in the window. Or under a door and air is going through.
- Gushes of wind between rocks in the high mountains.
- Ujjayi breathing, sirocco, and glacial winds . . .

### *Process and Stages*

Given the nature of this Voice Texture, I normally offer three different Body Sources for it. In each one of these, the glottal passage is going to be very narrow. Do not worry EVER about attaining a specific high sound. That is not the point. No particular sound might come out from your voice and that will be totally fine. Your only concern should be to create the environment of breath/Air sound on the hope that tiny "microscopic" sounds will salute you. Trust that those sounds will happen; you simply do not have a clue as to when they will.

Silence your left hemisphere and encourage your right one. Do not struggle and choke yourself making it happen. That it is not important. Why you play is what matters. The results are irrelevant. Some of you might experience these sounds immediately and others might take weeks.

The sounds are going to remind you of those high-pitched "peep," creaking sounds of a kettle with calcareous deposits in it, or dolphin squeaks, or a small balloon full of air allowing very little air to be released. I will not say it enough: to make those *exact* sounds is not important. What is important is for you to play and create an environment where those sounds might greet you. Then there will be a favorable environment for those sounds to appear and for you to experience them. Play and simply invite Air sounds to come to you and potentially any Image Words from your text, making sure to avoid throat tension.

*Always remember: Cool off your voice often.* If at any point in doing the work you feel light-headed, stop immediately. Sit or crouch down on the floor, allowing your head to get closer to the floor and breathe at your ease.

If/when you feel tightness in your throat do the following:

- Stop and run down several scales on "NG" and "NGA" to give you a good rest and provide a lower larynx.

- Sine wave on your Natural Pitch with "NG" as if you were rocking a baby.

## Corkscrew Experiment

1) Envision you are going to open a great bottle of wine. The cork, unfortunately, is going to be extremely tight to unscrew. Put the imaginary bottle between your knees and try to pull the cork up. Allow the sound of the tightness of the cork to be heard. Take your time. Use Shower Mouth and Tongue #3. Feel how the oropharynx and abdominal connection are being activated.
2) Before you feel tightness in your throat do the following:
   - Run down several scales on "NG" to give you a good laryngeal rest and lower placement.
   - Sine wave on your Natural Pitch with "NG" as if you were cradling baby to sleep. Relax.

## Baby in Cradle Experiment

1) Have the image of an infant lying down on its back in the cradle, after being bathed, pampered, and fed. The baby is in total bliss and playful. In nirvana really. Allow your body to sway from right to left as you grab your toes above your head. Your head is resting on the floor all the time. No tension. It's playtime!
2) Alternate between easy 20% short puffs of air and 40% sustained, longer ones. Use Shower Mouth and Tongue #3. Make sure you support your sound with lots of News.
3) These Voice Textures include the sounds that infants make around seven to nine months old, before they are ready to utter their first phoneme. Around this age, their larynx is still placed very high in their windpipe; it has not yet descended into what will become the laryngopharynx area. This is also the very moment when their ability to suck and breathe at the same time disappears. This process enables the infant to start saying phonemes. Both the nasopharynx and oropharynx participate strongly in this type of sound.

4) Before you feel tightness in your throat do the following:
   - Run down several scales on "NG" to give you a good laryngeal rest and lower placement.
   - Sine wave on your Natural Pitch with "NG" as if you were cradling baby to sleep. Relax.

### Nova Journey Experiment

You are going to be borrowing the Corkscrew experiment with a small variation.

1) You are going to use Shower Mouth and Tongue #3. You are lying on the floor, and you are going to use the right arm for "the journey." Left arm, left leg, and right leg are all lengthened and expanding from the center of your core with the feeling of centrifugal speed into the cosmos.
2) With each exhale, your right arm is going to move slightly further and further up and away. Think as if you were going to embark into a solar system light years' journey away, starting on Mercury and moving further and further away with each breath until you will reach Pluto.[5] Always keep your head relaxed on the floor, your shoulders on the floor until your arm reaches your right shoulder level; then, torque slightly and carry on. Every new movement synchronizes with a new breath. Maybe sounds come up, maybe not, but you keep feeding your action with News. Do not allow your Fictionalized body to collapse.
3) You can suspend the action of the arm any time; think of it as if you had arrived at a new planet, a black hole, or a Nova.
4) Feel free to exhale several times in the place you stopped before you start moving again towards the next "intergalactic destination." Remember to support your sounds with News.
5) Before you feel tightness in your throat do the following:
   - Run down several scales on "NG" to give you a good laryngeal rest and lower placement.
   - Sine wave on your Natural Pitch with "NG" as if you were cradling baby to sleep. Relax.
   - Rest your voice using your Natural Pitch.

### Imagery

- Do not aim to produce high-pitched sounds.

- Focus on creating an environment of Air/breath.
- Refer to the "Basic Air Thoughts" and each of the three Body Sources mentioned.

### Cooling Off

- Do a series of comfortable runs gliding down on "M," "N," "NG," and "NGA."
- Do the same but using trills.
- Revert to your Natural Pitch and hum with it.
- Hydrate yourself.

### Cornerstones

- Fiction and News.
- Alternate supporting the sound with and without your diaphragm.
- As soon as you lose touch with the sound, revert to your warm/cold breath, or ujjayi breath, to take a rest and regain your strength and flexibility.
- Remember this texture is not about producing specific sounds but about creating and building a breathy, airy environment.

### Listening References

- I recommend listening to high-pitched dolphin and whale calls, as well as the sound of newborn babies.

## Water

What excites me about this voice texture, similar to Air, is that it brings the opportunity to explore a different perception of time. If Air brings along the presence of ultrasounds, Water offers the opposite: "infra-sounds."

It offers a peek into our ancestral proto voice[6] with rich animal and visceral paralinguistic emotional material.

Water sounds imply a strong unleashing and an active **chthonic** release, the total opposite of what we saw in hypotonic Broken Earth. Sounds erupt in it like how I imagine magma or a primordial amalgam of matter with all different chemical elements would sound.

**178** The Foundational Pillars: The Body Sources

Water should rumble and quake as if excavating, dredging, and gouging dark, primal, **telluric**, longtime-forgotten sounds of our human experience, as if our psyche came to life.

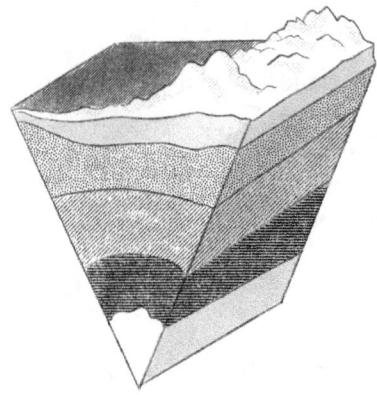

*Figure 6.7* Geological strata representing the excavation of the sounds needed for Water.

### Process and Stages

1) Start with *Nancy's Boots* on your Natural Pitch with basic vocal support in place (i.e., Tongue #3, Shower Mouth and 40% diaphragm support). Once you arrive back at your Natural Pitch, stay on it.
2) **Iron Man Hands Experiment**: add the engagement and awareness of energetic presence in the center of each of your palms. It should never be a pushing away, but rather you should be working with the feeling of leaning against a slight resistance, engaging with it like what we do with our heels leaning against the wall in the Astronaut's Experiment. This physical presence and awareness in your palms facilitate the triangulation and engagement with your pelvic center and "Dantien" all at the same time (Chi energy).

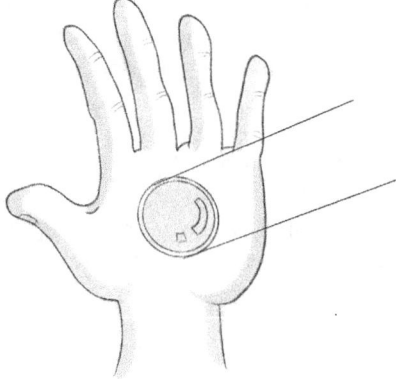

*Figure 6.8* Iron Man hand.

You are engaging your low abdominal musculature by having 40% with Shower Mouth and Tongue #3 and "Iron Hands."

3) With all these elements in place, start to go down the scale half-step by half-step until your sound will naturally break. Visualize the geological strata image as you go down each half-step. This should be done only at 40% in Shower Mouth. Resist the natural tendency to go less than 40% because it is rather difficult to maintain that percentage with such a low sound.

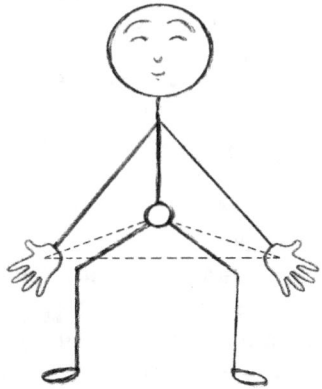

*Figure 6.9* Triangulation of Iron Man hands with the Dantien.

4) *Getting into the Komodo Dragon*: As the sound breaks, allow your torso to tilt slowly forward as you slowly transform into a Komodo Dragon. Maintain your lengthened spine as you do so. Avoid "guillotine" neck.

As you become a Komodo Dragon, be sure to have your buttocks and scapula at the same level, ending parallel to the floor and ceiling, as if someone were going to rest a breakfast tray on your flat back and have breakfast.

*Figure 6.10* A Komodo Dragon illustrating the primordial nature of Water sounds.

5) This Komodo Dragon image, the one of a huge crocodile or of a large iguana, is most conducive to this sound. End up with your spine *perfectly parallel* to the floor and ceiling. Once the sound settles with you, continue to go down half-step by half-step and play with it. Shift between paralinguistic material and the use of phonemes or Image Words from your text.

### *Imagery*

- Komodo Dragons, geological strata, murky bayou waters, ancient amphibian creatures, the primordial broth of Earth rich in microorganisms and substances, the goddess Kali, a drilling rig, excavating for gold or precious gems, going back into troglodyte ancestral times, a nomadic horde, deep freediving into the ocean waters, giving birth, etc.
- Once you "have" the sound, connect with other people making it. Listen and relate to each other. Use Image Words. Interact.

On all fours, move towards each other as if gathering strength for the horde. Lean onto each other, shoulder to shoulder, as if protecting or seeking collaboration with one another.
- Avoid imagery of charging, competition, violence, etc. to avoid overloading yourself with strong emotional responses stored in our "DNA memory."
- Rely on playing with positive, laudable, expansive, constructive, joyous, humorous, extroverted attitudes towards the other and the sound.
- Humor with this texture goes a long way. "Negative" emotions, unless they are framed within the context of a scene or monologue, can steer us in an undesirable emotional direction. Dr. Seuss' "Happy Birthday" short story is most suitable for this. Words like "frog, bro, grow, drog, Komodo, doorknob" can help you to balance the emotional output of this very strong lowest pitch organic sound.

### Cornerstones

- Fiction and News are crucial for this powerful voice texture.
- 40% vocal intensity all the way from beginning to end.
- Be meticulous with the whole process, especially when creating the image and transforming into the Komodo Dragon.
- Humor is most conducive to engage you with this powerful and strong sound without scaring oneself. Resist using negative emotions to start with as you get to know the Vocal Texture.

### Cooling Off

Because of the strong physical support and vocal energy that this texture demands, it is imperative that you cool off for your vocal health:

- Rest on your back aligning your body accordingly, arms at an inverted 10:10 by your side, knees up and feet on the ground, and allow yourself and your larynx to relax by using "NG" and "NGA" on descending glissando scales.
- The residual value of the sound you just produced on Water should offer you a very easy, comfortable, low, Natural Pitch Earth sound.

- Make sure that you "bank" on the Earth quality that results after the effort you had put into making Water sounds, as opposed to the Soft Wood sound that can easily appear instead in some people.
- Then shift to a series of comfortable runs gliding down on M, N, NG, and NGA.
- Do the same using trills by blowing out through your lips.
- Revert to your Natural Pitch – indulge in it and hum with it.
- Keep yourself hydrated. You used a lot of vocal energy. If you find your own means of being consistent with the sound using your own Body Source, please implement it your own way. As long as you follow these steps, you are doing the work. In other words, all roads lead to Rome; just make sure that you take the one you know best for you.

### Listening References

- Refer to in-class explorations to guide you in your auditory understanding of Water. For Body Source video clips, visit www.barrantesvoicesystem.com.

### The Scream

The Scream, while in daily life appears as an extraordinary and spontaneous element of expression, on stage must contain that very same element while also being delivered on cue. That is where the work resides. There is an art and technique for screaming, yelling, and shouting on stage. The key is to build *CONFIDENCE* in your ability to Scream and to assure it on demand. Based on the natural and organic way in which a Scream occurs in daily life, where there is a total synergy between necessity, vocal power, breath, and the action supporting the Scream, above all I recommend: the support of the diaphragm (40%), low larynx (Tongue #3), and the assistance of a specific, well-established, and rehearsed Scream Body Source. This, plus the consideration of adding both oro- and nasopharynx areas of resonation, will be paramount to avoid vocal injury and produce a healthy Scream.

## Process and Stages

1) Warm up and cool off before and after you Scream. Before you Scream, make sure that you tone your diaphragm and head resonators (explore Metal Voice Texture exercises which effectively include oro- and nasopharynx, in other words Tongue #1). You want your Scream to be as rich and expressive as possible. The Scream often occurs in the higher-pitched region of Metal.
2) Your Scream should definitely use a flexible Tongue #3 with Shower Mouth. Make sure your larynx is given the chance to rest, hydrate, and relax after shouting. Be specific with your image and a good 75% of the work will already be done.
3) Whether the Scream is short or long, the action (Body Source) supporting its vocalization should last the same time. There should be absolute *synchrony/redundancy* between what we hear and what we see (i.e., a one-second Scream will have a one-second action supporting it until the performer is ready to bring it to the stage without having to do the respective Body Source). Your physical action should be propelled as extroverted, expansive, explosive, centrifugal, open, large, and outward, versus introverted, constricting, implosive, centripetal, small, and inward.
4) An *image, an emotion, or a sensation* is a basic and fundamental element to trigger the action that will become the Body Source. Make sure you prepare that emotion.
5) The intensity and volume of a Scream on stage should never be the result of a release of 10/10 in intensity, but you should encourage instead a maximum release of 7/10, so that the audience does not witness the natural human limitations inherent to any performer. Sometimes it is useful to think of mumbling a word or a brief phrase "under" the Scream. The audience should not understand, nor even realize, that you are uttering a word or short phrase while doing so. That will defeat the very purpose of the Scream, which in essence, is a paralinguistic utterance even though it can be carried into words and phrases.

Keep in mind that sounds that release a certain sudden amount of energy, such as Broken Earth or Broken Metal, can be extremely useful tool for expressive Screams.

### Imagery

Pay attention and be mindful of the *plethora of screams* available to human emotion.

Know the origin and purpose of your Scream. A basic inventory might include:

- Joy, hurt, rage, anger, grief, pleasure, fear, Kiai offensive sound,[7] pain, surprise, disgust, madness, excitement, sadness, animal, etc.
- Be mindful of the pitch or pitch combination (the possibility of uttering several broken sounds at once) for the Scream you need to produce in question.

### Cornerstones

- News is vital for preparation.
- Centrifugal action.
- Use 7/10 rather than 10/10 intensity.
- Use low larynx on Tongue #3.
- Refer to Eckman's basic emotions **("F–A–D–E–S")**: Fear–Anger–Disgust–Enjoyment–Sadness, which you will find in more detail in Chapter 7 under *Creating a Task Experiment*.

### Cooling Off

- Voice your Natural Pitch on "M," "N," "NG," and "NGA" as if you were rocking and consoling an infant to sleep in your arms.
- Do a series of comfortable runs gliding down on "M," "N," "NG," and "NGA."
- From a fifth above your Natural Pitch come down half-tone by half-tone up to a third below your Natural Pitch. Do it on NG/Backyard, using *piano* or *mezzo forte* vocal intensity. Repeat three to five times, then do the same but starting on the octave or close to it and do glissandos down the scale. Repeat with NGA sound.

- Do the same using trills.
- Revert to your Natural Pitch and hum with it.
- Hydrate yourself.

**Listening References**

- *"The Unstoppable Tennis Grunt."*
- Sharapova grunts.
- Martial Arts Kiai: Sugino Sensei 10$^{th}$ Dan Master of Katori Shinto Ryu.
- Kendo World.

**Notes**

1 A **source point** describes the location where the primordial qi from the vital organs of the body assembles to get redistributed throughout one's body.
2 From the Greek word "psycho:" spirit (image, thought, idea) and "soma": body (emotion, sensation, perception).
3 Yes, this is in fact the very sound of the Cookie Monster from Sesame Street saying "Cookie!" and the famous "Whaaatssuuuup?" beer commercial guys – repeat these over and over. However, please note that some of the "Whaaassuuup" guys are producing a loud, high, tense, squeezed version of what we're looking for, which is to be avoided. "Broken Earth" is the flapping ventricular bands that create a "broken," tonally imprecise quality. Maintain that but with a lower, relaxed, hypotonic approach!
4 Lilli Lehmann (1948–1929) was a renowned opera singer & voice teacher who wrote the famous book *"How to Sing."*
5 This is a Mnemotechnic reminder for the planets in our solar system to assist you on your journey; "My Very Educated Mother Just Served Us Nine Pizzas" (Mercury–Venus–Earth–Mars–Jupiter–Saturn–Uranus–Neptune–Pluto).
6 **"Proto voice":** The raw voice and vocal material that exists in the human animal prior to its cultivation through the acquisition of language and socialization.
7 Kiai is the term used in martial arts for the energetic fighting spirit shouting sound that is released when attacking an opponent. Mental imagery is a vital factor that contributes deeply to the effective, and vocally harmless, execution of a shout.

# Chapter 7
# Training

## Grotesque

American Southern Gothic novelist Flannery O'Connor said that we may discover truth through distorting the known. We know that theater cannot exist unless the everyday nature of the voice/body behavior is altered. The voice–body training we do in class is designed to avoid mimicking the "ordinary" voice–body gestures we exhibit in our daily life. The fundamental idea is that from the moment you step into the classroom and take off your shoes, you tap into "someone else."

The goal is to sacrifice the ego, *eclipsing oneself*, remodeling and rearranging the daily voice–body by means of creating a **"grotesque"** type of training behavior.

Please understand "grotesque" as *distorted or unnatural in shape or size.*

"Grotesque behavior" helps build your own singular way of voicing and moving, while doing away with anecdote and illustration by creating a language designed purely for the stage.

We train the voice–body to create new Body Sources of sound (broadening the potential of the sound spectrum and vocal identities), but also to build a pre-existing vocabulary of sequences and gestures that we can call upon when we start our next training session or build a performance. The pallet of voices and actions implemented during training can be read as a specific blend of music, dance, painting, poetry, all of which are destined to eclipse the ego and everyday life. The gestures, actions, voice–body sources learned, and the training sessions represent the potential for geometric rather than arithmetic progression.

In this context, two plus two gestures do not make four but four hundred, since the gesture can be multiplied by means of changing the tempo, levels, directions, volume, geography, intensity, repetition, and isolation. The goal is to meet the demands for a broad range of aesthetic needs: realistic, naturalistic, symbolic, epic, abstract, metaphoric, hyper-real, etc.

You wish to create a world in which logic and causality do not prevail at all costs. A world like the ones of the dream world or the world of an infant, always telescoping between the symbolic and allegoric domains of reality, fantasy, and dream. A world of its own, drawing fuel from the long-lost territories of the right brain's hemisphere. These cryptic indecipherable worlds are often what enable us to understand and get on with our waking lives, rearranging our thoughts and creating order and meaning from so-called disorder.

Grotesque is born from the *constant switch and contrast* of voices and actions that defy linear thinking. It will manifest itself as you continue to borrow, isolate, edit, reduce, magnify, and change the voice–body gestures. It is important to feed and build a voice–body vocabulary to embark upon, as ceramist Stephen L. Horn says: "A journey with no destination that brings the soul near."

Never underestimate the audience's ability to recognize what lies between the lines of what they are seeing and hearing[1]. Often, actors think they have to "chew" and pre-digest the material they offer to their public. Audience members are sophisticated, however, and can draw their own conclusions. Let us not forget they are looking at the whole picture from outside, which is far broader than what we offer in a single scene. We performers must learn to abandon clichés and stereotypes to seek deeper means of expression to satisfy the audience's willingness to suspend disbelief from the weight of reality.

This training attitude and sacrifice mirrors Penelope in *The Odyssey*. She is the weaver who at night unravels the shroud she created to keep her suitors away. Think of the training session in the same way: a sacred space in which you do not want to be claimed, appropriated, or colonized by somebody else's model, and even less so by your own psychosomatic habitual patterns of behavior.

One of our important training goals as performers is to reveal our own singularity in the hope to attain artistic individuality. My mentor Masao Yamaguchi taught me that making theater is a way of creating a space that is denser than the space of daily life. There is a fair amount of truth considering performance as unproductive or an unnecessary ritual unless you saturate it with your own why. Only then does it become meaningful.

The "grotesque" is earned; it requires intensity and fervor through *selfless devotional activity*.

*Selfless* because the "grotesque" is not about "you" but about "it." It is about the voice–body task being executed.

*Devotional* because the "grotesque" requires an investment beyond reason – it is a way of life that the performer must master. Every master has trained for their calling. There is never mediocrity in mastery.

*Activity* is a task that simply understood creates voice–body physical actions, gestures, and tasks in the unique and personal signature of the performer. Be as specific as possible. Once we are committed to something, there is no need to question its outcome. Your activity must have unquestionable commitment with a clear aim to attain specificity, clarity, and liberation. You change your task as soon as your actions within the task become stale, uninhabited. It is about splurging, and spending energy lavishly, just like in a shopping spree.

This idea of "selfless devotional activity" is not new, many artistic masters swear by it including Zeami, Artaud, Jean Duvigneau, Grotowski, Tadeus Kantor, Robert Wilson, Reza Abdu, Roy Hart, Peter Brook, Jean Genet, Tadashi Suzuki, Pina Bausch, and Eugenio Barba to name a few.

The master knows that one must eclipse the ego. It is not about the artist but about their work. The ancestral performing traditions rooted in mythologies, rituals and folk celebrations surviving today understand this type of sacrifice.

We should be prepared to sweat and to share the jewel we forged with passion day after day as we gallop to reach the highest level of connection in what we are doing/making.

Maybe this can bring us closer to the unnamable.

## Building Your Training Session

Life is beautiful as it is and impossible to imitate, even though as humans we are always attempting to do so. Stage life is a purely man-made fiction, an "unpractical" space where anything can happen. Peter Brook, English theater and film director said that if in daily life the "if " is an evasion, onstage "if" becomes our fundamental truth.

Earlier in the twentieth century, Meyerhold made a clear distinction between the naturalist/realist canon, where synchronism between vocal and physical rhythms is guaranteed and the "stylized" canon of stage life is at the antipodes of real life.[2]

Using this latter approach, the performer gives up an essential part of their personality, their temperament, and their habits to follow other laws that are specific for the stage.

Training should be done regularly and for a consistent period, say at least 45–90 minutes. This way of working helps us to overcome physical and mental obstacles because it encourages the release of endorphins, creating a feeling of expansion, liberation, and euphoria. As we push our voice–body limits in training we can discover new ways of expressing ourselves free from the established thinking and social conventions we find ourselves exposed to in our daily life. When we train, it is important to discover and create our own singular language. We do this by constantly shifting, repeating, borrowing, isolating, and editing our vocabulary of gestural elements and tasks.

It is in executing our tasks that our fears, blocks, judgmental attitudes, and our own ego are let go, making us freer and more available for the creative voice–body process. Our multi-octave voice and the emotions that it evokes in the performer are enhanced by building a training type of behavior in which the sounds and actions employed have nothing to do with causal undertakings and procedures of the realistic world. In training everything should be subject to the constant shift of patterns, maps, plans and designs by the creation and accumulation of tasks that recruit the constant shifting between our right and left hemispheres.

### The Training Space: The Raft

If you consider the shared training space as a raft, you are immediately forced to be aware of and interact with your peers. Our "survival" depends on managing, distributing, and spreading the weight of the bodies evenly. If three out of five people are in one corner of the raft, the other two people must make sure the rest of the space is balanced. Not drowning is the vital objective, and the movement of one person has to be registered by everyone else. Equilibrium is the objective, and it can be interpreted in many ways, i.e., the number of people in a certain corner, differing height levels, weights, activities, etc.

### Creating Sound on the Raft

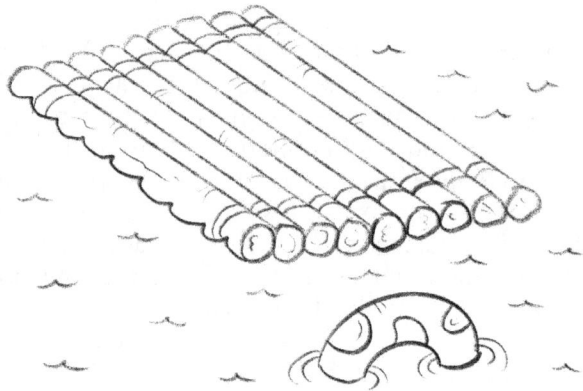

*Figure 7.1* Your training space experienced as a raft.

To avoid a cacophony of sound and to encourage connection and listening between the actors, performers should think of their voice as a call and response. This will help mitigate the "competition" between those training, and further avoid the sense of discord resulting from too many voices communicating all at once.

The four fundamental ways of generating sound are:

*Body Source*

This is described in detail in Chapter 6.

*Phonetic Chart*

Creating free-flowing body expressions for the sounds contained in the International Phonetic Alphabet.

*Singing*

This does not need further explanation.

*Paralinguistics*

Human utterances that communicate physical, emotional, cognitive, or perceptual states of being, i.e., the variety of "hmmmm" sounds, moans, groans, cries, whimpering, pleasure, coughing, laughing, sobbing, wailing, keening, screaming, etc.). Often in the vernacular these sounds are pejoratively referred as "noises."

## From "Raw to Cooked Sound"

The process of translating sound into text must follow a methodical step-by-step process. The training is the place to apply and remember all the voice–body sources you have learned. Now is the time to be ready to generate new gestures, tasks, movement phrases and new Body Sources. Your voice can only become freer. But how?

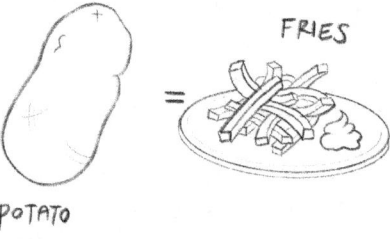

Figure 7.2 It's all about transformation....

Start by reviewing and applying the phonetic alphabet (consonant sounds and phonemes included). Explore these sounds as you move through space, using all the plosives, fricatives, laterals, affricates, and glides, giving them free, intuitive, body shapes and gestures.

Let these sounds flow freely from you until a clear body source appears. You will be able to identify the appearance of a Body

Source because of the energy it carries in the voice–body, because it galvanizes you and makes your creative imagination tangible in such moments.

Make sure then that you find a concise and repeatable way of executing that very body source several times in a row, so that you can memorize and "objectivize" it. If it is a vocal or paralinguistic body source sound, make sure you master how to translate the sound into the phonemes, words, and phrases of your text.

Further down, we will explore the following types of movement: *proverbial, intra-corporal, extra-corporal, and body source behavior.* Surprise yourself intuitively as you experiment with these elements. Avoid applying brain fuel and chatter. You want your ego out of the way.

**Eclipse** it and be one with what you are doing/making.

In training you too must sacrifice your daily body much in the way as the tightrope walker does in Genet's code of ethics.[3] If the tightrope walker does not "sacrifice" the self that exists in them before they set foot on the rope, the tightrope walker will never be able to emerge and traverse as an angel in the air above us without falling. It is that simple. And yes, you are alone in this. Alone as the tightrope walker, as the bull fighter in the arena, as an athlete on the court, but... in that situation you would transform yourself into a contagious magnet of inspiration, a danger to the norms of society and an extraordinary beacon of wonder and hope.

### Ways of Creating Movement on the Raft

*Proverbial*

This is based on the proverbs suggested in class. Approach it purely as intuitive gestural work. This will increase the ability to build a vocabulary during training.

*Extra-corporal*

The use of a ribbon (3 yards long by 1.5–2 yards wide) is a wonderful freeing tool to loosen the voice/body of the performer. It further encourages the apparition of non-daily ways of behaving, thus expanding the imagination.

Use the *ribbon* to build a repertory of specific actions that you can use as gestures to assist you with your text or singing material.

*Figure 7.3* Loosening the voice/body with the ribbon.

*Intra-corporal*

This way of moving originates from within the body. The quality of this movement comes from the training experiment of focusing and internalizing an imaginative sphere that can travel in the body at different speeds, density, and sizes from a small pin-point size to reaching even an eight-foot diameter sphere. The performer must follow the constant flow that the sphere will dictate as it travels "by its own will" in the performer's body as well as on the space of the raft; in other words, the performer is at the mercy of the movement of the sphere's.

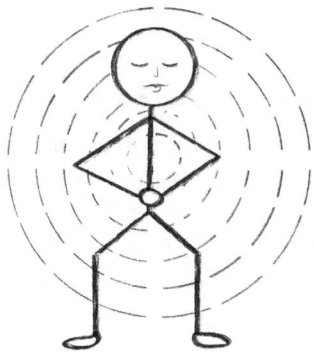

*Figure 7.4* Imagining sizes of the sphere emanating from your body.

*Body Sources*

Each body source has unique corporal, energetic, and sound properties, as described in Chapter 6. Body sources are a reliable and useful tool for generating specific actions and gestures.

**Discomfort**

As performers, we must be open to failure. As we try and try again, we fail again yet fail better. To feel discomfort in training is totally natural. To seek comfort, as we know it in daily life, is antithetical and counterproductive to our training. Etienne Decroux[4] would say that if your body felt physically uncomfortable when doing your work, you then stood the chance of maybe being right, or simply close to being right. There is nothing natural, organic, or effortless about the physical training of the performer. To eclipse one's biography we need similar energy to the one needed to ignite the fuel tank and the solid rocket boosters when launching the space shuttle.

The term "physical" includes the voice–body. Despite potential obstacles or difficulties during training, the performer must persevere. It can be useful to understand comfort as a type of satisfaction or relief. To rehearse is an unglamorous activity but by its sheer practice it will bring on eventual change and comfort. In English, to rehearse is synonymous with "to practice," "to prepare," "to train," or "to drill;" however, in French, to rehearse is *"répéter,"* which carries the idea of "to repeat" or "to ask again" and in Spanish, *"ensayar"* conveys the idea of "to try out," "to attempt," or "to experiment."

**Fundamental Training Protocols**

The research and writings of Italian theater director Eugenio Barba[5] have been a continuous source of inspiration in my work. In addition to voice and body gesture protocols, the following protocols are training guidelines that I have used with my students and actors over the years.

*1) Splurge On Energy*

Give. Spend energy repeatedly. Produce material without having a particular purpose in mind. Once you begin moving, stay moving for at least 45–90 minutes so that body chemistry can transcend the natural metabolic exchanges and release endorphins. You should be singularly focused on the task at hand. Staying in task will, in turn, free the imagination, thus bringing about "**news**." Be generous, be a giver, be a big spender. Binge, radiate, and squander – these verbs represent the opposite of our goals in daily life, where we aim to attain maximum results with minimum effort. To splurge is about the removal of daily attachments in hopes of finding a moment of visitation (inspiration). The rules that apply to the energy we display onstage are opposite to those of the market economy.

*2) Balance*

The actor's objective in training is to alter their natural balance. Unlike in real life, where we try to remain anchored and stand in place, in training you must allow yourself to finish a movement either before or after its natural duration. Human beings gravitate towards symmetry, stability, and equilibrium, and it takes effort to defy the pull of gravity. If the goal in daily life is maximum results with minimum effort, in theater the goal is to generate many actions instead of remaining in a perfect state of balance. Otherwise, the actor becomes static, and so the actor must defy the force of gravity and seek unstable balance, in a never-ending dance for balance. The goal is to be at ease with the uncomfortable. In this way, creating actions generates naturally dynamic situations that entertain the voice–body and spirit.

*3) Inertia*

Always resist inertia. Allow yourself to interfere with the natural inertia of completing an action. Stage movement is made for the stage – therefore we "block it." The natural inertia of daily actions does not work for the stage, because the stage is a larger-than-life and denser environment. Consequently, movement onstage must be consciously delayed, suspended, broken down, slowed, compressed, dilated, repeated, and edited so that we do not simply copy and transfer to it the actions of daily life. When done in this spirit, such actions and gestures contribute to the suspension of disbelief, stimulating wonder and reverie.

*4) Quantity Of Energy*

Unlike in daily life, inform your actions onstage by adding or subtracting energy. An action can be executed in many different degrees of intensity, between 1% and 100%, (i.e., the difference between grabbing a glass from a table at 50% or 90%). During training, do not maintain the same level of energy as your actions have in daily life. Do not "recognize" the body onstage; you have to be "excessive" in that you are constantly tweaking various energy levels. Either soften your movement, make it stronger, or find someplace in between. Although a performer is to some extent an acrobat of the soul, the performer's body does not benefit from the body of an acrobat. The point is not to build a muscular and acrobatic physique, but rather to cultivate a body that encourages flexibility, different hues, and musicality.

*5) Repetition*

This is a simple yet crucial notion for keeping the training fresh. Do not fear repeating an action over and over again. Repeating an action or gesture breaks down its logic and naturalness.

*6) Isolation*

Focusing attention on one specific area or part of the body is useful, not only to create awareness but also for expressive material. Being selective and invested in a particular anatomical area opens the area and expands it in novel ways.

*7) Borrow*

What happens on the "raft" – the training space – is subject to a constant give and take between performers. This is what is meant by borrowing: if your colleague does something at the other end of the room that inspires you, borrow the gesture and feel free to transform it. Allow it to become yours – there is no stealing between performers, only borrowing.

**Eclipse Yourself: The Task**

Jerzy Grotowski, Polish director and theorist, who was a pioneer of experimental and physical theater, said that theater held the power to traverse the borders that separate you and me.

An eclipse can be defined as the partial or complete obscuring of one celestial body by another. An eclipse is a momentary, transitional, and impermanent event. After an eclipse, the luminosity of the eclipsed celestial body returns to its original state. The audience is not looking at you the performer, but rather your transformation into what you have become.

*Figure 7.5* The phases of the eclipse.

Eclipsing the ego is an effective way of forgetting about self-consciousness, especially in a métier where the ego is often prone to inflation. There is a very simple technique to attain this: having a specific task at hand, and if you do not have one, create one. When a performer feels "put on the spot" when first encountering new material, they might be nervous and not know what to do. This is the time then when it becomes important to create a task to allow the performer to overcome their nerves, self-consciousness, and judgment.

A task should be something physical, based on a straightforward action that can be easily executed. The more physical and specific the task, the easier will be to make a connection. Since we are speaking purely of a physical action, there is no need to worry about anything other than its immediate justification. As soon as the task is combined with the delivery, both the imagination and the body will be affected. Connections will begin to appear, thus releasing the actor's ability to improvise. We are talking of an action to fall back on, a point of departure. The point is: the action remains clear, specific, and predictable, so that the ego can be eclipsed. Once the performer has executed the task, they must find a way to justify the action within the performance's context. This requires perseverance, for the performer must find at least one justification, even if it changes from one day to the next, for the seemingly random action they decided to execute.

This experiment serves as a stepping stone. The idea is simply to get the blood moving and the head out of the way, having a physical task at hand that can support performative material. Trust this. There is no other way to uncover the right action for the material. What is important is to begin. Find a task. Do it NOW. Solidarity between action and any specific material (the play, a scene, etc.) requires time, direction, research, focus, and many hours of rehearsal. In working with the script and the director, the actor will slowly find the appropriate tasks for a given scene.

The performer must avoid the following questions:

- How am I coming across?
- Am I doing it right?
- Is this what the director wants?
- Is this in keeping with the scene?
- Am I going to be called back?

These types of fears can only destroy the performer's confidence. They restrict and put into question the actor's creativity at the moment it is most needed.

The idea is simple. For example, let us imagine you decide to purchase an airplane ticket online.

1) You go to the website and enter: From... To...
2) You decide about the dates and click: Done.
3) You select your departure and return flights, then you move to the fare option.
4) You book it and enter all your personal and financial information.
5) You click the final: Buy.
6) And you get on happily with the rest of your day.

In this example, there is no point in asking:

- Did I press the keys on the keyboard well?
- Was my typing rhythm a good speed?
- Did the algorithm like me?

All that matters is that the task is completed: you purchased an airplane ticket. Theater is about action in connection to words. During training, or when the performer is unsure or in a rut, they must have the same attitude as when making their previous online purchase. There is no time for worry, for psychological stress or self-policing; what should prevail is only to have a clear plan to implement step by step with simple physical tasks. Having a specific physical task will take the performer out of their head.

When a writer has writer's block, for example, they do not stop writing. A writer simply keeps putting pen to paper, writing whatever comes to mind, and only in this way can the mind become free flowing once more.

### Creating a Task Experiment

Create a simple physical task and include at least three actions:

1) Walk five steps forward.
2) Touch the nape of your neck with one hand.
3) Go down to the floor and look right.

This experiment has two goals:

- Use the support of a physical action to deliver the performance ("getting out of the head").
- Find a way to connect the material with the associated task.

In the classroom or in the rehearsal I often ask my students to create a task on the spot to apply the material we are working in class that day even if it is only for 30 seconds' improvisation.

If you add to the task the remaining integral elements of the performing plan you end up creating a Playing Module:[6]

| | |
|---|---|
| **T**ime Frame | 60-90 seconds < beginning-transition-end |
| **P**rerequisites | Fiction & News |
| PLAN OF **C**ontent | Text, song, or paralinguistic |
| PLAN OF **A**CTION | Task |
| PLAN OF **S**OUND | Voice Textures |
| PLAN OF **E**MOTION | Emotion |

*Figure 7.6* Utilize this Playing Module – **TP CASE** – to organize your performance elements.

## On Connection

*Figure 7.7* Representation of connectivity and connection.

Maya Angelou adopted the famous Chinese proverb that states, *"A bird does not sing because it has an answer. It sings because it has a song."*

Anybody can make a sound, say a text, move, or... but that does not mean that they are a singer, an actor, or a dancer. We should perform not because we can but because we have something to say. For our skills to transcend to an audience the interpreter must be not only in *connection* with itself but also with the material at stake. *Connecting* with what one gives voice to is at the root of success.

When you are *connected*, you are never worried by the outcome, or by the definitions and the labels that control the market economy (when I was a young man in the sixties, we simply used to call it "capitalist values"). When you are creating, you are fully connected, immersed in the flow of making, undivided, free of brain chatter and judgment.

On stage we strive to make sense, to be present in the moment. We are simply saying/dancing/singing/making in that moment, so that you transcend the limitations that the daily lifetime frame imposes on you. You reach in front, behind, right, center, or left but also to above and below.

We strive to create even though we experience life as something deeply beautiful. We do so because we know there is a link with life that we are still missing. We gallop after it hoping to attain it and to relate to it. That is why we create and create over and over again. We want to connect with ourselves, with the other, with "it."

*Connection* in the performing arts today is vital not only because there is so much more "maya," in the sense of our current virtual reality, than ever before around us, but because unlike other art forms, in the theater we have the profound privilege of sharing simultaneously time and space with others.

We come together to the same place. Today that is a huge "act." When I use the word "connection" I think of it as in the Sanskrit meaning of the word "yoga"[7] – a union of breath, body, and mind.

When this amalgamation takes place, audiences come to see who you have become because then you represent inspiration, vision incarnated, a beacon of hope. In that moment you are giving the audience wings on which to soar, you are unfolding them, and broadening them. Only at that moment "you" have become an artist, not before then.

**Snow as Connection**

March 2015. Koyasan Mountains, Japan.

It has been snowing outside the monastery since early this morning. I had to open the sliding window and hear the muffled sound of snow falling. I look again at the mountain in white and suddenly, I realize how much snow has to do with connection. In Japan, snow and its whiteness speak of mourning, and of the final transformation, death.

These free-flowing topsy-turvy particles of frozen water (like our words on stage) dance in the wind with the possibility of sticking to each other and to the surfaces of things, to the ground...

It is certain that they will only stick if the right combination of the temperature, the intensity of the flakes and the time lapse of their falling happens to converge. Only then those flurries will become the "continuous sheath" that is essential to snow and makes snow, snow. Nothing is as it appears. Just like theater. Anything exposed to the snowflakes will be covered and eventually connected. Snow, like voice textures and acting needs time to lay down, to settle, to stick, to join, to integrate.

In Spanish we say "la nieve esta cuajando." "Cuajar" in Spanish means to join, to gel, to link, parts of a liquid for transforming it into a solid substance. In French one says "la neige prends, elle tient," snow takes, grabs, holds. In English, the "snow sticks." No matter what in each of those languages there is that sense of "clinging/joining." This is exactly what happens in rehearsal. We hear and "rehear" the words of the play again and again. And just like gradual and gentle flurries, at the end of the process, there is the linking arc of things together, fusion of elements, the real connection.

The performer's tacit wish for its audience is pure: "I want to connect with you." It is certainly not about making sounds and throwing words at the audience, getting rid of them as quick as one can say them. Anyone can do that. The wish for the performer is to open one's interior so that they can reveal to the other (the audience) something that is important, matters and is close to the performer. Snow, like performing, is mysterious. It erases the inherent limits and definitions of the daily world as we know it, breaking its boundaries and creating new meanings.

Snow, like theater, is a mesmerizing spectacle for all. While it lasts, it binds together those things that were physically separate and different from each other, softening their edges, fusing them, and creating new contours, extending its limits, blurring them, equalizing them, connecting them all as far as the eye can see into *one single* extended sheath, one single coat, one covering layer, just like imagination. Snow glows just the same as when sound, breath, word, body, and mind are connected. Snow, like performing, is ephemeral: a stage in between the fluidity of water and the solidity of ice. It only lasts so long before it melts and reveals again the prosaic life forms and materials of the slush of life. Whether we look at it from above or from below, seen from without or from within, snow, like acting, is all about connection and being connected.

*Figure 7.8* Snow erasing the boundaries of individual objects, connecting them together.

### The Right Temperature in Two Stories: Stew and Fever

Snow can only stick if the ground temperature where it falls is below 32° Fahrenheit (0° Celsius). Only then, those separate water fragments will accumulate and get ready to erase and transform the daily world with its preexisting differences, as we know it. The curious paradox is that even though what we see is only in "neutral" white, that sheath is fully charged, like poetry, with the potential of new possibilities and meanings.

This is not so different from the performer, needing to bring together all different elements of his craft to make sense and create meaning. The idea of "right temperature" has led to the goals I set for my work in class, the rehearsal, and the performance. In learning, if there is not "fever" in the space we are working or in the body, the new material cannot sink in, cannot be metabolized, chiseled, and inscribed in the flesh. That inner heat, that inner fever of the performer is what unleashes transformation. If there is not enough heat, there is no possible change. Just like making a stew.

## 204 Training

When you cook a stew, you want to use the tough, large and lean cuts of the meat to sear and simmer for a long time so that in combination with marrowbone they will "shine" in your mouth when your guests taste it. Do you know why you want those cuts in your stew? Those pieces of meat contain collagen,[8] a very rich protein in *connective* tissue, and when simmered at the right temperature, it breaks down making the meat tender, tasty and rich. That is exactly what you want your performance to be: a succulent rich nourishing substance.

If the words, the sounds, the emotions, and the actions of the performer are not cooked well enough and fully incorporated into the broth (of the spirit), they are just that: simple, uncooked ingredients unlikely to be digested and metabolized.

### Hand in Hand

Now that you have your text integrated with the voice, you need to make sure that your delivery remains connected with your words.

For me as a performer, words are like when I am strolling in the park or the mountain hand in hand with someone I love. It is a matter of coupling the effort of being together at the same time and in the same place. Your words, your actions, your mind, and your spirit walk hand in hand to create that ideal moment of connection. This in turn creates intimacy, and for us on the stage, a moment of true theater.

My great teacher and mentor Marita Gunter said once to me, "Remember that the beauty of the world and the beauty of the word is in its mystery, not in its explanation."

*Figure 7.9* Mother and daughter walking hand in hand.

This image found me while editing this chapter and studying, at the same time, the materialistic minutia of the DMV 2021 California Driver's Handbook. I found it to be such an eloquent symbol of the "Hand in Hand" story I just wrote...

The crosswalk in the picture is no other but the "performance," bridging our two realities: on the one side of the road, before crossing, is the present, the daily. On the opposite side, the future, the imaginative, the created one.

The mother holding the hand of her young daughter is the "performer." The young daughter holding the hand of her mother represents that brand-new, delicate "material" (all those actions and words we block and learn by heart) that need to be integrated by the performer.

The crosswalk of the picture acts in the same way as the "hashi-gakari" in Japanese Noh Theater: a bridge connecting the world of the spirits (the room of mirrors, "kagami no ma") to the world that gets revealed and unfolds on earth, the stage witnessed by the audience.

For a safe crossing of the road two things have to happen: the older and the younger have to hold hands and avoid running. There is no other way.

## Notes

1 In his book *The Empty Space*, Peter Brook speaks about the fringe of this no man's land between the actor and the audience, which is at the core of true communication.
2 Refers to the "Biomechanics" chapter on "Meyerhold: The Grotesque" of *The Secret Art of the Performer* by Eugenio Barba and Nicola Savarese.
3 This is what Jean Genet's grapples within his work *The Tightrope Walker*.
4 E. Decroux (1898–1991) was a French actor from the Vieux Colombier School. He devoted his life to create and develop the technique of "corporeal mime." His art form represented an innovative drastic departure from the classic anecdotal and representative notion of mime and pantomime.
5 Eugenio Barba is an Italian author and theater director based in Denmark. He is the founder of the Odin Theater and the International School of Theater Anthropology, both located in Holstebro, Denmark.
6 The acronym for this Playing Module will be **TP CASE**.

7 The etymological meaning of "yoga" is the joining of two things together. The word derives from the Sanskrit verb *yuj*, meaning to join or fasten two things together.
8 Collagen: a structural protein of connective tissue. From the Greek *kola* "glue" + *-gen* "giving birth to."

# Conclusion
## The Universe in a Lid . . .

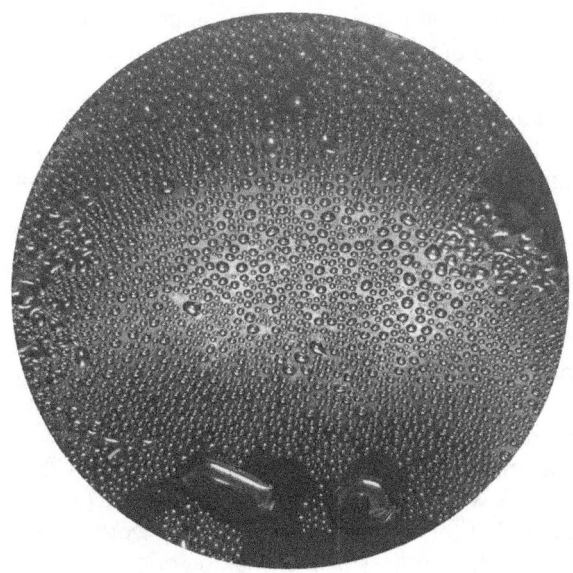

*Figure C.1* A photograph representing the myriad of worlds existing in one's voice.

Years ago, sipping some tea one morning after kyudo practice, my teacher shared with us a wonderful story about his mother. When he was young, she told him how important it was before drinking his murky miso soup at the table, to do the following:

> Gently take the lid of the bowl and turn it upside down with a delicate yet deliberate swift motion. After that, pay attention to

the clear beads that have gathered in the black lacquered surface of the lid while the miso soup had been covered.

There was something very poetic and extremely real about this story: the simple fact that it all takes place in no more than a three inches wide concave lid. What a paradox!

I could not wait to try this on my own. So, as I carefully removed the lid off my bowl, I noticed two things. First, I noticed the cloudy and muddy substance of the broth in the bowl, and second, the innumerable number of transparent specks of condensation that had assembled on the lid. Those translucent droplets sparkled against the deep black lacquered lid just like a faraway galaxy of planets in the cosmos. The tiny glassy dewdrops could not exist without the turbid miso broth. So simple, yet so astounding.

Each of those specks represents for me the innate, mysterious, impermanent, insubstantial, elemental, emotional, immaterial, individual, ancestral, specific, cultural, and natural sounds that each one of us carries inside.

My teaching journey over the last 40 years has always been driven by my wish to find and break down the best, most reliable ways to connect with that myriad of specks of identity and of experience I just mentioned. Giving voice to those connections not only empowers us as individuals, but also makes us soar as actors. It enables us to travel further into that universe.

My goal in building the Barrantes Voice System has been to provide actors with a variety of tools and rigorous means to help them to connect their internal and external worlds on the stage, as they pursue the endless task of making one's voice visible.

*Pasadena, Summer 2022.*

# Glossary

**Acoustic Coupling** When the pharyngeal cavities are properly aligned and "tuned" for resonation of the tone, *Acoustic Coupling* occurs between the vocal cords and the resonator.

**Amber Light** Borrowed from the image of the caution symbolized by an amber traffic light, this expression commonly used in my system refers to the moment in one's breath when the brain sends the message, "It is time to let new air into your body, take a new breath."

**Arytenoid** The arytenoid cartilages or arytenoids are a pair of pyramid-shaped structures that sit on top of the cricoid cartilage of the larynx. Their function is to approximate the vocal folds, to tense them or relax them.

**Biographical, Biography** The history of a person's life. All those qualities, conscious and unconscious elements, idiosyncrasies, etc. that make a person the person they are. I often insist on how essential it is to erase one's biography so that we can incarnate "the other" on stage.

**Body Chatter** Those involuntary muscular actions of our daily way of using our bodies that happen when we do not pay full attention to the experiments we are implementing i.e., fidgeting. The muscles we are trying to cultivate in each experiment get distracted by our quotidian, habitual movements, making the work inefficient.

**Body Source** As its name indicates, the Body Source is the geographic location in the body where a specific sound can be found and produced. This specific location or physical gesture in the body of the performer acts as a direct line to unlock a specific Vocal Texture.

**Buddha Belly** A relaxed, soft, round, and potbellied low abdomen that is often depicted in the images of contemplative or joyous Buddhas.

**Cante Jondo** In Spanish, it refers to the deep, profound, and full of pathos quality of Romany and Andalusian popular flamenco singing styles. In English, it could be translated as "deep singing."

**C-A-S-E of "The Tee Pee Fades the C-A-S-E"** This mnemotechnic tool helps the performer remember the four fundamental plans necessary to build a performing module:

Plan of Content (text or song), Plan of Action (gestures/actions used), Plan of Sound (Water, Earth, Wood, Metal, Air), Plan of Emotion (Fear, Anger, Disgust, Enjoyment, Sadness)

**Chthonic** Understood as something pertaining to or having to do with the earth and the underworld.

**Concave** The surface is hollowed out or rounded inwards, like inside a bowl, as in the case of a cave.

**Conditioned Breathing** This is the ideal breathing we want to practice supporting and strengthening our work on stage without hurting ourselves. I call it *conditioned* because there is nothing natural about it. It comes to life by sheer practice and training.

**Convex** The opposite of concave, a surface that is curved or rounded outward.

**Cricoid** A fundamental cartilage of the larynx with a signet ring-like shaped cartilage that is larger in the back where the arytenoid cartilages sit. It is located below the thyroid cartilage and above the trachea.

**Crystallized** This refers to the state of the pupils when they become rigid, fixed, frozen, and lifeless, instead of relaxed, soft, engaged, or involved in the act of looking.

**Dantien** The Taoist concept of *Dantiens* as an energy center is not so different from the concept of chakras in yoga. They both consider this place as a seminal location in the body where *prana* (life-force, or breath) is saved and collected. The term

*Dantien* is also equivalent to the Japanese word *hara*, which means "belly." In Chinese, Korean, and Japanese traditions, the *Dantien* is considered the physical center of gravity of the human body and the source of one's Chi (qi) or internal energy.

**Duende** The *duende* that Federico Garcia Lorca shared with us in his essay "In Search of Duende" has nothing to do with the literal English translation of the word duende, which means "elf." In *duende,* there is not magical thinking or any presence of "elves." *Duende* has everything to do with that which is *sacred*. It is unnamable. I interpret it as that pinch of the soul that wakes us up to a higher sphere of experience and perception. *Duende* is fleeting and ephemeral, just like the voice. It appears when we experience certain works of art or privileged moments of life that are deeply and indescribably charged with beauty, pain, and energy. Those emotions galvanize our being to the point of throwing our sense of self into a free, vertiginous fall that marries heaven and hell at once, leaving us in awe, perplexed, and in need of recovery.

**Eclipse** An eclipse is a momentary, transitional, and impermanent event. After an eclipse, the luminosity of the eclipsed celestial body returns to its original state. For the actor, it is imperative to eclipse one's ego. Eclipsing the ego is an effective way of forgetting about self-consciousness, especially in a métier where the ego is often prone to inflation.

**F-A-D-E-S of "The Tee Pee Fades the C-A-S-E"** This mnemotechnic tool refers to the five basic emotions that I use in the classroom to create performing playing structures:

Fear – Anger – Disgust – Enjoyment – Sadness

**Fiction** One of the two prerequisites of the performer onstage. Fiction is a vital element for the actor. It is a shift of energy that takes place inside the body. Fiction is a subtle energy in the performer that cannot be confused with the person performing it.

**Glottal Fry** Or "vocal fry" is an uneven staccato sound produced by compression of the vocal folds by means of using very little air flow. The result is a sound like popcorn popping, or a crackling, creaking, rattling, or broken type of sound.

**Gravidness** Understood as something with gravity. In the context of our work, it is the force that attracts the pelvic area and abdomen toward the center of the earth. In other words, gravidness means heavy, with weight, full, loaded. The etymology of this word comes from the Latin *gravidus*, "loaded, full, swollen, pregnant with child."

**Grotesque** Understand this concept as: *"Distorted or unnatural in shape or size."*

The goal of the performer is to sacrifice the ego, eclipsing oneself, remodeling and rearranging the daily voice–body by means of creating a "grotesque" type of training behavior. A "Grotesque behavior" helps build your own singular way of voicing and moving, while doing away with anecdote and illustration by creating a language designed purely for the stage.

**Hypertonic** One of the three basic muscular tones, characterized by high muscle tone state of being.

**Hypotonic** One of the three basic muscular tones, characterized by low muscle tone state of being.

**Image Words** The words in a text that suggest images, sensations, perceptions, thoughts, and ideas for the person saying them. It includes nouns, verbs, and adjectives but never articles, prepositions, or conjunctions.

**Inner Tube** An image that I often use when referring to inhalation to encourage a 360° natural expansion of the abdominal area.

**Japanese Noh Theater** Noh Theater is one of the oldest traditional surviving forms of theater from Japan, dating back to the fourteenth century. Its structure is based on song, acting, and dance. Its repertoire has five categories: god, man, woman, mad-woman, and demons. The use of the voice is highly stylized and in combination with a choir and musical instruments, it evokes the world of ghosts coming to earth to tell their stories using masks and opulent silk costumes. Buddhist themes are contained often in the plot of the plays.

**Kaspar Hauser** He was a German boy who apparently was raised in total isolation, deprived of language itself, and then suddenly appeared at a Nuremberg square one day armed with only a single sentence (that he apparently did not even understand the meaning of). He became the ward of a well-known socialite lawyer, who educated and socialized him. For further references on this historical figure: the film "The Enigma of Kaspar Hauser" (1974) by Werner Herzog; *Gaspar* by Peter Handke; the French text "Caspar Hauser" by Thierry Garrel and Vania Vilers; "An Account of an Individual Kept in a Dungeon" by Anselm Von Feurbach; "Caspar Hauser: Oder, Die Trägheit Des Herzens" by Jakob Wassermann, translated into Spanish by Jorge Miracle Arola.

**Lips Trills** A basic vocal warm up and conditioning exercise to help the closing of the vocal folds, stabilizing the larynx, air flow pressure, and diaphragm/breath support. It relaxes facial and neck muscles, as well as vocal tension.

**Métier** A French word that means vocation, calling, trade, and/or profession.

**Multi-Octave Vocal Range, Multi-Octave Voice** Pertaining to more than one octave. An *octave* being an interval in which the higher note is twice the frequency of its lower note. "Multi-Octave," understood as that "arsenal of sounds," that exists uniquely within each human voice, beyond the comfortable average octave that we use in everyday life.

**Nancy's Boots** This experiment borrows its name from Nancy Sinatra's famous song, "These Boots are Made for Walking," which opens with one of the most famous bass lines of pop music. In our system, we borrow the same idea of the bass line going down the octave by using the intervals to tune our voices and achieve musical accuracy, combining it with playfulness.

**Nasal Quality** The desirable timbre or quality by the resonance of the sound in the nasopharynx. This quality is optimized by the proper placement of the tongue and use of the soft palate while using the sounds: M, N, NG.

**Nasality** Undesirable, exaggerated nasal twang, timbre, or quality in one's voice due to impeding the free flow the flow of air through the nose resulting in congesting the sound.

**Natural Pitch** That note in your Earth voice that acts as the base or "home" where to build the Multi-Octave voice. That comfortable, specific note to each individual is the result of a natural, non-projected sound, using Tongue #3 at 40% on Shower Mouth.

**News** It is one of the two prerequisites of the performer on stage. I constantly request from my students and performers to "give me NEWS." If you are in the business of telling stories, it is imperative that whatever you do on stage is "connected" to a specific image, emotion, sensation, perception, feeling, thought, or idea linked to what you are expressing. News is that: an ephemeral, renewable, ever-present, constant flow of information (intellectual, sensorial, perceptual, experiential) that has to be communicated.

**Organic Breathing** This is our daily way of breathing. This breathing is based on the observation of the breath of a naturally healthy infant being properly looked after, well fed, nurtured, played with, and pampered.

**Paralinguistics** The area of communication that does not use words. In other words, it is non-verbal, such as pitch, volume, stress, accents, utterances, screams, laughter, cries, coughing, and all the human utterances that communicate physical, emotional, cognitive, or perceptual states of being. These can include a variety of "hmmmm" sounds, moans, groans, cries, whimpers, pleasures, coughs, laughs, sobs, wails, keens, screams, etc.). Often in vernacular, these sounds are pejoratively referred to as "noises."

**Perineal** Relating to the perineum, the area in women between the vaginal opening and the anus, and in men the scrotum and the anus.

**Pitch** The quality of a sound related to the frequency of the vibrations of the sound waves producing them. The highness or lowness of a tone: the place of a single sound in the complete range of sound.

**Proto Voice** The raw voice and vocal material that exists in the human animal prior to its cultivation through the acquisition of language and socialization.

**Psychotropic** A psychotropic chemical element is a substance that changes nervous system function and results in alterations in perception, mood, consciousness, cognition, or behavior.

**Relative Position** The position in the body where the skeletal and muscular forces are properly distributed and aligned. Proper verticality encourages muscle tonicity and relieves constriction of the body and throat. There are many different terms to describe a "neutral body position." In the Barrantes Voice System, I call it **the relative** because individuals are different in their own constitution. Fundamentally, we are talking of a parallel, second ballet position in which the head, shoulders, pelvis, knees, and feet are aligned.

**Roy Hart Theater** Its founder Roy Hart (1926–1975) took the lead on the work, that his teacher Alfred Wolfsohn had previously created, researched, and developed. In the mid-sixties, with the presence of nearly 40 people, the Roy Hart Theater was created. In July 1974, the company moved to the South of France, to the Chateau de Malerargues, an abandoned hotel in the heart of the Cevennes mountains on a former seventeenth-century silk farm in the Languedoc-Roussillon, near the towns of Nimes, Avignon and Montpellier. It was also near an important center of "La Resistance" in France during World War II. I joined the RHT in 1974 and stayed in the company until 1990. These will forever be unforgettable years of learning, education, and vocal development.

**Shingon Buddhist School** This school of Buddhism was founded by Kūkai (774–835), posthumously known as Kōbō Daishi, a Japanese Buddhist monk, calligrapher, and poet. The school places great emphasis on the true meanings of Buddhism, as well as the ability to achieve Buddhahood in this life. Buddhahood can only be apprehended through the artistic representation of prescribed rituals regarding the three esoteric mysteries of: the body, speech, and mind, hence the use of mudras, mantras, chanting (Shomio), and meditation.

**Shomio** The Japanese Buddhist ritual and devotional chant used by the Tendai and Shingon schools. Shomio employs a pentatonic scale and is characterized by long extended bent notes, followed by a rigorous breathing technique.

**Shower Mouth** The natural shape that the mouth happens to do when we take a shower to avoid suffocating us by the water droplets coming into our noses. This natural relaxing of the jaw is at the basis for a healthy voice production. It is a drop, never a voluntary, forceful opening of the mouth.

**Sine Wave** Understood in the context of my system as the visual representation of how the sound is being modulated, oscillating like a sound wave, or like the visual representation of the heartbeat signals in an electrocardiogram.

**Source Point** In the healing system of acupuncture, a "source point" describes the location where the primordial Chi (qi) from the vital organs of the body assembles to get redistributed throughout one's body.

**Spelunker** Or a speleologist (in professional terms), is someone who explores and studies natural and wild caves. In the context of my system, a spelunker is someone who explores and examines one's voice. I often visualize the body as a mountain containing innumerable inner paths leading to underground landscapes and formidable geological formations like stalagmites, tunnels, caves, springs, underground rivers, sink holes, etc. All these different types of geological formations are metaphorical representations of our voice and Body Sources.

**Subglottal Area** The area of the larynx below the vocal folds until the trachea.

**Suriashi Noh Walk** It is the sliding walk in Japanese Noh Traditional theater. The heel of the foot of your back leg does not get off the floor as it steps forward but slides on the floor instead. Prior to accomplishing the full step in front of you, the toes and the ball of your foot will be off the floor slightly before the whole foot rests on the floor to allow the other foot, now behind you, to take the next step in the same manner.

**Tailor Position** Describes a basic yoga sitting position on the floor with your spine lengthened and your legs comfortably crossed close to your body.

**Telluric** Related or pertaining to the earth, terrestrial, earthly.

**"The Tee Pee Fades the C-A-S-E"** This mnemotechnic tool helps the performer to remember how to include all the fundamental elements necessary to create a performing module. In other words: a time frame, two prerequisites (fiction and news), the five universal basic emotions (fear, anger, disgust, enjoyment, sadness), a Plan of Content (text/song), a Plan of Action (gesture/actions), a Plan of Sound (Water, Earth, Wood, Metal, Air), and a Plan of Emotion (FADES).

**Three Pillars** The following constitute the three pillars of the Barrantes Voice System: Fiction, News, and the Body Sources related to the five Voice Textures: Water, Earth, Wood, Metal and Air.

**Tonic** Of the three basic muscular states of tonicity, tonic is the ideal one because it offers vigor, well-being, energy, and strength.

**Voice Texture** Any of the five voice qualities, colors, or textures used in the Barrantes Voice System, i.e., Water, Earth, Wood, Metal, Air.

# Index

*Note*: Endnotes are indicated by the page number followed by "n" and the note number e.g., 36n4 refers to note 4 on page 36.

2001 Experiment 120, 127

Abdu, Reza 188
Abraxian voice 13
acoustic coupling 30–31, 52, 134–36
acoustic levels 129–33
Air *see* Body Source
Alexander Technique 52
*Alice in Wonderland* 24
amber light 89, 118, 127–29, 140, 157–60, 209
American Dance Festival 7
Angelou, Maya 200
apophenia 27n2
appoggio 69, 84, 141n1
Archipelago Theatre France and USA 7–8
arsenal of sounds 2, 15, 213
Artaud, Antonin 13, 188
arytenoid 46, 209–10
Astronaut Experiments: Against the Wall 61, 69–70; Astronaut 61, 84–85, 178; Slow-Motion Spacewalk 72–73; Standing-Up 71–72
Axes Experiment 53

Baby in Cradle Experiment 175–76
Ballet Bar Experiment 136

Barba, Eugenio 77n2, 188, 194, 205n5
Barrantes Voice System 6–7, 10, 15, 42, 94, 142, 208, 215–17
Barthes, Roland 10
Bartoli, Cecilia 162–64
Bausch, Pina 5, 188
Big Ben Bell Strikes Experiment 128–29
biography 17, 19, 102, 152–56, 194, 209
body chatter 65, 209
Body Source: Air 33, 40, 47, 172–77; Broken Earth 50, 148–54, 177, 184–85; Broken Metal 33, 169–72; Broken Wood 160–61; definition 142–44; Earth 144–46; Epic Hollow Wood 162–64; Lyric Hollow Wood 164–65; Metal 33, 165–71; Soft Wood 158–59, 160–61, 182; Strong Wood 154–58, 160; Water 50, 177–82
Botero 146
Broadway 7: experiments 89, 118–119, 126–127; position 179
Broken Earth *see* Body Source
Broken Metal *see* Body Source
Broken Wood *see* Body Source

Brook, Peter 23, 76, 188–189, 205n1
Buddha belly: definition 59–61, 85–86, 210; experiments 66–75, 84–88, 102–103, 138, 145–146; inner tube 212

California Institute of the Arts 1, 7
cervical: area 54, 121, 139; belt 29, 30, 44, 52–55, 61, 71, 97, 100, 140; column 37; vertebrae 31, 37, 52–54, 97, 116
Chi energy 64, 77n9, 178, 211, 216
Chi Kung 145
Circles Experiment 53
Cloud Viewing Experiment 54
concave pelvis: definition 68–71, 210; experiments 85, 126–27, 146, 149, 163
conditioned breathing: definition 62, 79, 82, 210 experiments 31, 66–71, 83–94, 102, 107, 116–17, 137
convex pelvis 68–70, 85, 210
Cookie Monster 50, 148–54, 185n3
Corkscrew Experiment 175–76
Cow and the Halloween Cat Experiment 81–82
Creating a Task Experiment 184, 199
cricoid 45–46, 209–10
crystallized 24, 28, 210

Da Pacem Cordium Experiment 115
Dantien 63–66, 77n9 n. 9–10, 210; triangulation 179
Dantien Call Experiment 76
Decroux, Etienne 194, 205n4
Diaphragm Stretch Experiment 61–62
Driving Experiment 135–36
duende 13, 16, 211
Duhhhh Experiment 99
Duke University 7, 18
Duvigneau, Jean 188

Earth *see* Body Source
eclipsing the ego 15, 18, 186–88, 192–99, 211
Eolo 173
Epic Hollow Wood *see* Body Source
epiglottis 45–46, 77n4
ethmoid 35
être bouche bée 43, 97
expiration 60–61
expressionism 14
extra-corporal 192–93

F-A-D-E-S 184, 199, 210–11, 217
Ferrier, Kathleen "Ombra Mai Fu" 164–65
Fiction: body source experiments 142–85; definition 16–23, 211; three pillars 142, 217; TP CASE 199, 217
foci lengths 32
Foo Dog Experiment 137–140
Four Times Eight: concept 120–21; 4 x 8 experiments 122–23
frontal sinus 34
Frontal Stretch Experiment 55

Gauthier, Brigitte 5
Genet, Jean 188, 192, 205n3
Gills: conditioned breathing experiments 82, 85, 88–92; with Foo Dog 138; intercostal awakening 101–09; sound grounding 56, 60–61, 69–71
glacial 173–174
Glass of Water Experiment 20–21
glottal fry 160–161, 212
von Goethe, Johann Wolfgang 13
Grotesque 169, 186–88, 212
Grotowski, Jerzy 188, 196
Grounding: Pelvis and Feet Calls Experiment 76
guillotine/flamingo neck 29, 71, 118, 140, 180
Gunter, Marita 204

Hall, Edward T. 129, 140n4
Handke, Peter 12, 213

hara *see* dantien
Hart, Roy and Roy Hart Theatre 5–7, 15, 142, 188, 215
head resonators: definition 32–37; laryngopharynx 45–47; nasopharynx 39, 170, 213; oropharynx 39–40; paranasal sinuses 34–35
Horizontal/Transversal Placement Perception of Tongue #1, #2, #3 Experiment 115–116
Horn, Stephen L. 187
Huxley, Aldous 13
hyper-real 166–167, 187
hypertonic 22–23, 61, 86, 171, 212
hypotonic 21–22, 61, 148, 177, 212

ideal gaze building 28–31
image words 76, 212; body source experiments 146–82
Imagining Lifting Experiment 135–36
inner tube *see* Buddha belly
inspiration 57, 59, 78
intercostals *see* Gills
intra-corporal 192–93
Iron Man Hands Experiment 178–82
inverted 10: 10: body source experiments 145–49, 162–63, 181; breath experiments 85–92, 102–08, 118, 127; imagery 146; sound grounding 43–73

Japanese Noh Theatre 8, 11, 15, 141n7, 205, 212, 216
Jung, Carl 5, 13

Kali 180
Kantor, Tadeus 188
Kiai 184–185
Kinesthetic Diaphragm Experiments: Friction-ing Hands 89; Pelvis Rudder 89–90; The Piston 93–94; The Wok and Frog 90–92

laryngopharynx *see* head resonators
Larynx Experiment 47
Lehmann, Lilli 166, 185n4
Lessing, Doris 21
lip trills 119–120
Listening to Your Shoulder Experiment 54
Lorca, Federico Garcia *see* duende
low abdominal breathing 41, 85–89
Lyric Hollow Wood *see* Body Source

Massaging Your TMJ and SCM Experiment 44
Masseter Experiment 44–45
Matterhorn-Cervino Tongue Experiment 116–117
maxillary sinus 35
mesentery 62–63
Meyerhold 189
Modernism 4
Motokiyo, Zeami 8, 13–14, 133, 141n7, 188
Mouth #1 with "N" in preparation for Tongue #1 or "Front Yard" Experiment 36
Mouth #2 with "M" in preparation for Tongue #2 or "Home" Experiment 36
Mouth #3 with "NGA "in preparation for Tongue #3 or "Backyard" Experiment 36–37
multi-octave 2, 4, 6–7, 10–15, 189, 213–214
Munch, Edvard *The Scream* 43–45

Nancy's Boots 120, 126, 178, 213
nasal cavity 33, 35, 39
nasality and nasal quality 33, 166–68, 213–214
nasopharynx *see* head resonators
natural pitch: body source experiments 142–85; breath experiments 99–136; definition 214; sound grounding 36–47

News: body source experiments 142–85; breath experiments 68–129; definition 23–27, 195, 214; three pillars 142, 217; TP CASE 199, 217
NG and NGA: body source experiments 142–85; breath experiments 68–139; definition 36; relaxing jaw 43
Noh Theater 8–15, 72–73, 141n7, 205, 212, 216
Nova Journey Experiment 176–77

O'Connor, Flannery 186
*The Odyssey* 187
Off Broadway 119
Opening Dantien Experiment 64–65
organic breathing 79–80, 214
Organic Breathing Experiment 80–81
oropharynx *see* head resonators

paralinguistics 161, 171, 191, 214
paranasal sinuses *see* head resonators
pelvis 65–70
pelvis rudder 89–90
Pelvis and Psoas Release Experiment 75
Pelvis and Psoas Tonification Experiment 73–75
perineal 65–66, 214
Perineal Call Experiment 75–76
pharyngeal constrictor muscles 38–41
pharynx 37–41, 45, 124, 173
phonetic chart 191
Pigeon's Neck Experiment 54
proprioception 28, 36–37, 46, 89–95
proto voice 13, 177, 185n6, 215
proverbial 115, 192
psoas muscle 66–68, 73–75

Red Light/ Green Light 16–18
relative position: body source experiments 149–70; breath experiments 80–89, 106, 117–128; definition 94–97, 215; sound grounding 29–55
Rumi 94

sagittal view 39, 46
Sanskrit 88, 201, 206n7
Sargasso Torso Experiment 106–07
scaffold 100, 115–17, 144
Scaffolding and Monitoring of the Shower Mouth Experiment 99–100
SCM 44
the Scream 182–185
Sculptor and Clay Experiment 20
selfless devotional activity 188
Shingon Buddhist sect 2, 8, 15, 124, 215–16
Soft Wood *see* Body Source
Shomio 2, 8, 15, 120–29, 215–16
Shomio on the Fifth Experiment 125
shower mouth: body source experiments 145–85; breath experiments 84–141; definition 97–98, 216; sound grounding 36–71
Shower Mouth Shakes Experiment 99
sirocco 172–74
solar plexus 55–56, 93
source point 142, 185n1, 216
Spanish Cante Jondo 8, 15, 210
spelunker 14, 216
sphenoid 35
Sposa 162–64
Strong Wood *see* Body Source
suriashi Noh walk 72–73, 216
Suzuki, Tadashi 188

Tabletop Against the Wall Experiment 109–10
tailor position 19–20, 66, 102, 216
Tailor Position Experiment 19–20
Theater of Cruelty 13
thorax 51–59, 62, 86, 95

three pillars 142, 217
three mouth positions *see* Tongue #1, Tongue #2, and Tongue #3
three muscular states *see* hypertonic, hypotonic, and tonic
thyroid cartilage 40, 47–48, 100, 210
Tibetan chanting 51
TMJ 42–44, 99
Tomatis, Dr. Alfred A. 52
tonic: body source experiments 145–71; breath experiments 73, 118–19, 127, 135; definition 21–22, 61, 217
Tongue #1 36, 111–16, 167–83
Tongue #2 36, 112–16, 128, 163–65
Tongue #3 36–37, 70, 85, 101, 112–29, 146–84, 214
TP CASE 199, 210–11, 217
Trajectory of the Eyes Experiment 31–32

Ujjayi breath 172–77
Understanding Kinesthetically the Notion of Fiction Experiment 19
Union Jack Experiment 66

ventricular bands 50–51, 148, 185n3
vocal cords, vocal folds 46–51, 119, 141n5, 209
voice texture 33, 144, 217 *see also* Body Source
*Voice Made Visible* 2, 8, 14–15

Water *see* Body Source
Weil, Simone 17
Wilson, Robert 188
Wolfsohn, Alfred 5, 215

Yamaguchi, Masao 8, 188
Yes/No Experiment 53
Your Shakespeare Works "On You" Experiment 88
yugen 13

For Product Safety Concerns and Information please contact our EU
representative GPSR@taylorandfrancis.com
Taylor & Francis Verlag GmbH, Kaufingerstraße 24, 80331 München, Germany

www.ingramcontent.com/pod-product-compliance
Lightning Source LLC
Chambersburg PA
CBHW070604300426
44113CB00010B/1393